MOVEM

STARFISH

UNLEASHING THE
UNSTOPPABLE
MISSION OF JESUS

MOVEMENT

DAN
GRIDER

PUBLISHING

MISSION OF JESUS

STARFISH MOVEMENT
UNLEASHING THE UNSTOPPABLE MISSION OF JESUS

Scripture taken from the New International Version®, Copyright © 1973, 1978, 1984 Bible Publishers. Used by permission of Zondervan Bible Publishers.

ISBN: 9781520114439

Cover Design: Tyler Goode
Editing: Rodney Arnold, Diane Rodocker, Dan & Becky Riemenschneider

Table Of Contents

STARFISH

Introduction

What is a Starfish Movement?

It was one of those moments when everything seemed to stand still. The late afternoon sun was just kissing the horizon. I sat astride my surfboard 200 yards off the Southern California coast. I was staring out to sea mesmerized by the spectacular sunset that dust from the Mount Pinatubo volcano created from its recent eruption 7,000 miles away.

The setting sun bathed the sky in a stunning show of radiant warm colors of gold and orange. It didn't matter that I was missing potential waves. The moment was all encompassing.

As I sat suspended on my surfboard I noticed that 10 feet beneath the surface of the Pacific was a false floor of colorful creatures. I had never seen anything like them before. They were brilliant. Perhaps they stood out because the celestial sky-scape above me was reflecting the perfect hue to light them up. Whatever the reason, the creatures fascinated me. The aquatic floor of color was a collection of five-armed urchins floating in mass as far as I could see.

I later learned more about the sub-surface sea carpet which, it turns out, was a mass collection of starfish. The starfish is an amazing creature. There are nearly 2,000 species living in the world's oceans. They use a variety of spectacular colors for camouflage or to scare off potential attackers. They often move in large clusters

The starfish was designed with multiplication in every cell.

Even though a starfish has no head, it has everything necessary to survive. It has no central processing system. All of its systems are distributed throughout its entire body. In fact, the major organs are replicated throughout every arm of the creature.

If you cut the starfish in half, you'll be in for a surprise; the animal won't die, and soon you'll have two starfish. It is amazing that an entirely new starfish can be formed from just a small portion of another. The contributing starfish will soon regenerate a replacement for its severed limb.

The starfish was designed with multiplication in every cell. That means a starfish will often reproduce in a situation that would otherwise kill another animal. This multiplication quality is the definition of resilience.

A coastal fishing village in Australia faced a crisis. The starfish population was growing at an alarming rate. The massive numbers began to overtake the coastal inlet and destroy the coral. So a group of motivated locals decided to eliminate all the starfish along the Great Barrier Reef. A group of divers began to slice up every starfish they found—unaware they were causing the starfish population to explode.[1]

This reproductive quality in nature is a perfect parallel to what occurred in the explosive discipleship development of the early church. There, success came from the movement's decentralized nature. There was no geographic center, no institutional focus, and after Jesus' resurrection there was not a single central leader. In fact, the church experienced explosive growth for nearly 300 years.

Jesus established the Church to be a starfish movement from the beginning. This season of growth saw a motley band of peasants reproduce until nearly half the known world had become Christ followers.

Certainly a collection of leaders emerged over time. Every starfish movement must have a catalyst. Catalytic initiatives can only grow into a movement when there is a reproducible process that is not dependent on the presence of a single

[1]Ori Brafman, Rod A. Beckstrom, *The Starfish and the Spider: The Unstoppable Power of Leaderless Organizations*, Penguin Publishing, London, 2006 p. 144.

leader. Leadership bottlenecks occur when one person is essential to every decision and all forward movement.

Starfish movements often become even more explosive when the catalyst is removed and the power shifts outward. This shift of influence and power from the centralized nerve center to the outer concentric circles will make the movement nearly unstoppable.

Early Jewish and Roman leaders consolidated leadership. They depended on a focal leader and a highly institutionalized system. They wrongly assumed that the movement Jesus started depended on a lone leader, that if they just removed Jesus, His movement would die. They had never seen a starfish movement.

"The blood of the martyrs was the seed of the church." Tertullian

They expected the unruly, disorganized collection of Jesus followers to scatter when they threatened persecution and death. But the more officials opposed and punished them, the more they reproduced. The movement was unstoppable because it was decentralized and simple. Simple creatures like the starfish can reproduce rapidly. This is a foreign concept to those of us who have become accustomed to a complex church culture.

In the book of Acts, the early church seemed to multiply more rapidly when it was persecuted. In the second century, on the heels of Roman oppression, Tertullian observed, "The blood of the martyrs was the seed of the church."

The starfish movement Jesus launched has the capacity for explosive reproduction. The exact same elements present in the first century are present today. We must learn to release the elements that will result in rapid discipleship multiplication. If we are going to engage in the mission Jesus gave us, we need to learn from the original starfish movement.

VERSION ONE
THE ORIGINAL STARFISH MOVEMENT

We read about the "starfish movement" when we open the Gospels and the book of Acts. We will call this, "Starfish Movement, Version One." The word used to describe the small clusters of disciples was the Greek word *ekklesia*, which means "a collection of those who have been changed by the work of the Spirit of God to reproduce disciples." Jesus intended that this movement would rapidly expand to "the ends of the earth" (Acts 1:8).

The genius of the New Testament church was the lack of a central earthly leader after Jesus' ascension.

As this movement rolled out, it had many different updates and shifts that became part of Starfish Movement Version One. Philip's encounter with the Ethiopian on the Gaza road was a

Starfish One expansion event. It was another Starfish moment when the headquarters moved from Jerusalem to Antioch.

Then the Spirit's prompting to expand to Macedonia was a further ripple. The book of Acts details the combination of starfish expansions that occurred under the direct leadership of Jesus as He worked through the Holy Spirit to change the world. The Spirit of God was empowering and leading, but followers were not being motivated by a single catalytic earthly leader making decisions and establishing the vision. The Starfish Movement was rapidly reproducing leaders.

VERSION TWO
THE ANTI-MOVEMENT

The New Testament is packed with amazing stories of life change. This can't help but awaken something inside us. What created such an explosive radical movement? Why was their experience so full of life change and the authentic work of God?

We look at the current church culture and see an entirely different picture. Most Christians today live out a humdrum, habituated existence compared to the Christ followers of the first century. When did we lose our grip on Starfish Movement Version One?

The New Testament church was simple and reproducible. This movement experienced explosive growth until Constantine, the Roman emperor, embraced Christianity for his own purposes and institutionalized all things church. The only way to kill a starfish movement is to institutionalize it and merge the church with an intricate governmental system.

Complex things grow slowly and often are crushed under the weight of their own burdensome frame. Simple structures are reproducible and can multiply rapidly. Compare a starfish to a whale. Some starfish can reproduce after eight weeks because they are simple creatures. Whales on the other hand are much more complex and aren't able to reproduce until they are 15 years old.

Jesus launched a simple starfish movement. Leadership was decentralized and had a simple unifying mission. They were Jesus followers, period. The life of Jesus that was lived out in them reproduced life everywhere they went. As a result it reproduced quickly. The Jewish and Roman cultures were more like the complex orca. Ironically the American church has become like the involved institutional systems of Jesus' day.

Roman leaders eventually realized their approach toward quelling the New Testament church movement didn't work. Each emperor was a vicious persecutor of Jesus' followers, until the Roman empire came under the rule of Constantine. The movement had reached the tipping point in less than 300 years, and he recognized it. There were more Christ followers in his empire than pagan emperor worshippers.

Constantine made a shrewd political decision to wrap his arms around the movement. Instead of increasing persecution, he did what most leaders do; he added complexity to the once lean and nimble organization. In doing so he neutralized the starfish qualities of the movement.

In one instant, Starfish Version One went from the underground fringes to the main stage and everything changed. Jesus' followers were celebrated instead of persecuted. They became the focus of the Roman culture. An all-out effort was made to collect any relics or possessions of the once ostracized followers of Jesus. Shrines were built to honor the fallen martyrs that past Emperors had killed. The culture shifted its zeal for emperor worship to apostle worship.

Rome smothered the starfish with institutional affection. The movement's swift growth quickly stalled. The church immediately became less about rapid, organic multiplication of Spirit-filled followers who would gather the *ekklesia* (small communities of believers) and more about the process of building a legacy. The modern church is still a product of the version two shift from 1,700 years ago.

The New Testament church was simple and reproducible.

The American church culture with its events, programs and buildings came from Version Two Christianity. Over the years we have upgraded the institutionalized, anti-movement version of the church. The upgrades became more about style and form and less about multiplication. In most places we have not been able to move back to the principles of the starfish movement

The Church has focused on *ecclesiology*, which is its own practices, more than on relationships. The relational community of believers, or *ekklesia,* was at the heart of the starfish movement. Upgrades have tried to match the church to popular culture. When the church fully embraces the culture it struggles to keep its distinctive. Mission drift is inevitable. Prophetic voices occasionally emerge to call the church back to its mission and purpose, all the while we sit adrift in the ocean of culture unable to paddle toward progress in any direction.

Spiritual awakening moments are nothing new. The first and second great awakenings were significant moments. It looked like the church would be able to break the grip of the Version Two anti-movement, but once awakened, it tended to slip back into the institutional grip.

> *"The original starfish movement was snuffed out by complexity of the version two church."*

The focus of the Church for the past 30 years has been about updating its presentation and music style. The shift to embrace "contemporary worship" was just another cosmetic upgrade for a stuck Version Two church. Superficial adjustments will never move the Church out of Version Two. Different service styles, whether liturgical, traditional, revivalistic or charismatic make little difference.

Preaching styles won't do it either. We have run through the cycle of preaching fads. Pastors have tried topical sermons, inductive sermons, expository messages, and high-church homilies. They remain incremental adjustments – like painting your old car instead of replacing the engine. People are often passionate for a certain style, but the truth is, most fads did a reasonably good job of sharing truth concepts. Some were better than others, but most stayed true to the biblical text.

New plug-ins or software patches won't alter the Version Two shift that Constantine initiated 1,700 years ago. Christians argue over form and style with misplaced passion. The truth is, we all are missing what Jesus came to give us. Most of us live in Christian communities that are distracted and off mission. We are not experiencing a starfish movement.

There is little value in searching for a better model of the version two church.

In the past some Christians have pushed against modernism. They thought that eliminating all that is culturally modern from their church environment would usher in a return to the days of the first century Starfish Version One. The Amish and the Mennonites took that path. They are now in steep decline. Antimodernity is not the answer. The good news is that something exciting interesting is happening in poor countries of South America and Africa and in nations like India and China.

VERSION THREE
THE STARFISH MOVEMENT

We must realize that it's impossible to return to Starfish Version One. God's movement in history is like the movement of traffic on a crowded freeway. It is impossible to stop and back up. The only direction we can move is forward. And yet, there is a major spiritual shift happening in the world.

Superficial tweaks will not fix what is broken in the version two church.

Neil Cole introduced this concept in his book *Church 3.0*. Cole believes we're in the midst of the next major shift. Look globally at what the Father is up to. We are seeing a Starfish Version Three movement breaking out in new ways. China is a great example of starfish multiplication.[2]

The average church planter in China is an 18-year-old girl who is minimally educated. The average American Christian already knows more than this young church planter, which proves that simply possessing biblical information does not create a disciplemaker. She lives annually on what the average American church planter makes in a single month.

The difference is that she already has begun to lead a movement of reproduction that has resulted in a living room full of new converts. These new converts are hungry to know more about

---

[2] Neil Cole, *Church 3.0*. Jossey Bass, San Francisco, 2010. p.7

this person they have begun to follow named Jesus. This is radically different from what most of us experience in American Version Two churches.[3]

What is happening in China, and in parts of Africa and South America, is a categorical shift. This is more than the American house church emphasis. House church worship can be another upgrade to the Version Two church. In many cases the house church is a smaller more intimate Version Two model of the more institutional lethargic American church.

In these countries people in the starfish *ekklesia* that Jesus spoke of are experiencing a genuine movement. If this shift is to happen here, we will need to alter almost everything we understand about what it means to follow Jesus and learn the essential principles of how to be a part of a rapidly multiplying *ekklesia*.

MY STARFISH ENCOUNTER

I first saw the starfish movement at work when I was a young adult living internationally where I encountered Christ followers who had been radically changed by their encounter with Jesus. These Christ followers were not focused on doing church, but rather living for Jesus. When I returned to the States, I eventually discovered a group that was living in a similar way. They were different from any other group of Christians I had met in the States. I didn't know it then, but I was being drawn into the starfish movement.

---

3 Neil Cole, *Ordinary Hero: Becoming a Disciple Who Makes a Difference*, Baker Publishing, Grand Rapids, 2011 p. 71

These experiences were stimulating, but before long I had to get a job and become an adult. My degree was in broadcasting, so I worked my way into an on-air job as an afternoon drive radio personality in Lexington, the sixty-first media market in the country. It wasn't Los Angeles, but it was a start.

It seemed that most people in the entertainment culture were angry at the church and many were resistant to the Christian message. I was surrounded by a group of people who regularly mocked Christians and the church. This didn't bother me much because I identified myself as a Christ follower not as a church person.

We must learn to identify ourselves as Christ followers instead of church members.

I was new to the process of discipleship. I knew very little about how it all worked. I chose not to spar with those who were openly hostile but decided to ask questions. It was only a few weeks before those I worked with started asking me questions on the very topics they regularly mocked Christians about. I told them I didn't have many answers because I didn't. I was just starting my journey. I had not yet been trained theologically, so I had not been shown how to crush a discipleship culture with "proper theological answers." Instead, I invited them to join me to look for answers in the Scriptures.

I was shocked by how many of them wanted to look into the Bible to find answers to their questions. I showed them what I knew. I began to meet with one or two then three—this small group was joining me to look for answers in the Bible. I didn't realize I was doing discipleship. No one had told me I should make disciples—this was a natural outgrowth of what was naturally happening in my life.

The number of guys who wanted to talk about Jesus progressively grew. I didn't realize I was starting a starfish movement. I was simply sharing with them what I was learning. I was growing in knowledge and I was building a biblical worldview. It was shocking how quickly the guys were embracing the Bible. It was impacting their language and the decisions they were making. During this time several of them gave their lives to Christ and began to disciple other radio people. I loved what was happening. This had been so satisfying that I wanted to take the next step—whatever that was.

I sought out some Christian pastors and asked them what my next steps should be. They told me to leave the radio station and move to Louisville so I could attend the seminary they had attended. Some also suggested I leave the secular radio station and work at a Christian station. I wanted to learn as much as I could, so I did what they recommended. I assumed those pastors knew how to continue this contagious starfish discipleship culture.

When I relocated to Louisville, I had to find a radio job. I walked into one of the first radio stations that had a contemporary Christian format and got a job that day. This also was a move up in the radio world. I had gone from the sixty-first media market to the forty-fifth. I enrolled at Southern Baptist Theological Seminary and was on my way to learn how to make disciples like Jesus did.

Throughout my educational process I became skilled at answering theological questions. I was learning a new way to live. I was becoming a church person. I had a new vocabulary. I was unaware that leaders of local churches had to learn a new language besides Greek and Hebrew. I was learning to speak in church and theological ways. I was sounding more formal and educated. I didn't realize I was becoming a professional Christian. They showed me there was an entire professional field for a properly trained church person. This professional Christian thing was much more vast than I had known before. It was at times overwhelming. The only thing missing was the joy I had when I was discipling those "crusty foul-mouthed" radio people.

The starfish movement that Jesus initiated, often is turned into an overly structured, institutional machine.

I was becoming institutionalized. There wasn't a master plan for me to become a non-reproducing institutionalized Christian. It was a collective thing. I slowly became like all the other Christians I knew. The church does this to so many young Christ followers. Without meaning to, the church culture with its structure and formal institutions can crush everything reproductive out of new Christ followers.

I continued this institutional church process for years. I earned my masters degree and doctorate. I even taught pastors at Golden Gate Theological Seminary how to move followers who began as potential viral disciple makers to become institutionalized church members.

This is not intended to be a criticism of Christian education. I learned much from my professors. This is an observation of something much larger. It's about how the American church has taken the highly reproductive starfish movement that Jesus gave and turned it into an overly structured institutional machine.

It took me 15 years to recover from my "churchification" process. This recovery only happened because of the pain and disappointment I was experiencing as a frustrated pastor. I realized that I had to get back to the vibrancy that I saw during the early days of my Christian journey.

While I was working as a DJ, I had seen what it looked like to make disciples who reproduced other disciples. Since that time, I had become a pastor who was spiritually sterile. I had planted a church in Southern California, but I was frustrated that there was no discipleship multiplication happening in that church. I didn't like what I had become. This disappointment provided the motivation to rediscover how to make reproducing disciples.

The Father had initially allowed me to experience a discipleship culture that was multiplying. I simply had to return to what I had known to do in the early days. It helped that I moved far away from a church-infested culture to rediscover how to make disciples.

*It takes time and intention to recover
from excessive "churchification.*

My discipleship journey was one of rediscovering the starfish movement. Most of us early in our Christian journey have the ability to become a reproducing disciple. We're sidelined in the process of connecting with church people. I am like many others who were attracted initially to the person of Jesus but wound up exchanging Him for church life.

If we can change this process for new Christ followers we will see a starfish movement emerge. This process sounds easy but cultural Christian behaviors are deeply ingrained in our American culture.

*The Christ followers in a starfish movement
will naturally connect with each other and
the world in a more authentic way.*

If we are to launch a starfish culture that can produce vibrant reproductive Jesus followers a few essential elements have to be in place. We'll discuss those elements and describe how you can launch a starfish movement.

A starfish movement must be based around what God has already begun to do in your life. People ask me how the starfish movement works and I describe a process in which every person can be involved in the significant reproduction of disciples. This process starts with learning how to initiate effective one-on-one spiritual conversations.

They often say, "So you are teaching people how to do evangelism." I explain that what we call evangelism is not found in the Bible. The New Testament followers of Jesus didn't force a script on someone with the desire to get them to pray a "sinner's prayer" which would be followed by a new believers' class, baptism and a life of volunteerism in a sterile institution.

Jesus taught His followers how to engage in conversations that included a thought-provoking question and a story of how their life had been radically changed.

The power of the starfish movement is in learning to connect with people in a spiritually authentic way. As the relationship develops, the disciple will learn to have conversations that expose the life change that the Holy Spirit has created because they have had a personal encounter with the living Jesus. The goal of the spiritual conversation is to identify individuals who are disciple-able. A disciple-able person is someone who will simply take the next step of advancing his or her relationship with Jesus. Jesus began by discipling His followers without any rush to formalization or institutionalization. He simply let the process unfold. This process is what creates a starfish movement.

We can change our approach to church growth and become more reproductive by using Jesus as our model. The starfish movement is about becoming a refocused Christ follower. The key is to embrace a different way of thinking about discipleship that allows the Spirit of God to lead you to the people that He wants discipled.

Jesus launched a movement that has rippled throughout the world for 2,000 years.

How did Jesus launch a movement that rippled throughout the entire world until it got to you and me? We often make excuses for the challenges we face, yet Jesus launched His movement under the weight of the tyrannical rule of Rome. Early adopters of Jesus' way faced intense oppression that came from the established Jewish system. They had none of the things we think are associated with Christianity or church. They had no Bible, no buildings, no services; they didn't even do Bible studies.

When I present the concepts for launching a starfish movement to leaders and pastors, I ask an important question: What was Jesus' strategy for making disciples? Most will respond that He discipled them by spending time with them, teaching them, and doing life with them. These answers describe Jesus' approach during the instructional phase that preceded the launch of the movement. I remind them that their answers simply have described Jesus and His disciples rhythm of life.

They haven't identified Jesus' strategy to launch a starfish movement. For many years I have taught this to hundreds of groups and seldom have I found a US church leader who can describe the strategy that Jesus employed.

If we can't articulate the strategy that Jesus gave us for multiplying disciples, we won't be able to accomplish His mission on earth.

Our struggle to identify Jesus' strategy to make disciples should concern us. If we can't answer this most basic of questions for a Christ follower, it is certain that we will not be able to make disciples who reproduce disciples. Because we struggle with this foundational element we will be left out of the starfish movement Jesus created.

This realization creates tension for Christians. Tension is a critical element in the strategy that Jesus used to cultivate His disciples. Jesus knew that without tension the selected disciples would probably never embrace His new Kingdom culture. Starfish movements are built from disciples who have sufficient tension to learn the strategy of Jesus. They also need tension to follow the Holy Spirit.

Next during the conference, I ask participants to stand and place their smart phones and wallets on the table. I then ask them to follow me to the front door. I pause at the door to explain that they have been "punked." They thought they were coming to a training event, but they have been set up. Instead of attending the conference, I explain that we are going on a trip and that I have arranged for a bus to take us to the nearby towns and villages. Before we load the bus there is one stipulation: This is only for those who have been Christ followers for 18 months or more.

I remind them of when Jesus used this approach to train His disciples; He invested a year and a half with most of them. I remind them that they will need to recall all that they know about how Jesus made disciples to complete this exercise. Those who meet the criteria and who are willing to take the next step are paired up and assigned a town.

Then I tell them the bad news: There are no meals prepared for them and no place for them to sleep that night. The primary assignment for them is to find a "person of peace," and remain with that person for the next several weeks. By this time most participants understand the point of the exercise. They realize there is no bus coming and their anxiety fades.

Tension was a key ingredient that Jesus used to make disciples.

They get a first-hand view of how difficult it must have been for Jesus' 12 disciples when He gave them the assignment, and then removed all of the items upon which they usually relied. Jesus clearly designed this exercise to move His followers out of their comfort zones. It was designed to do more than simply get their attention; He established the primary strategy for launching the starfish movement.

Most who do this exercise come to realize they are excessively dependent on their wallets and smart phones. With those two items most of us have the tools necessary to resolve the housing and food tension that the disciples faced. It is clear that starfish movements are launched by leaders who learn to follow the Holy Spirit's leading.

Jesus introduced His followers to a situation that would produce tension so they would learn how to make disciples and thereby launch the movement. They were also required to apply everything that they had learned up to that point.

These disciples would have to do three things. First, they would have to follow the leading of the Holy Spirit as they took the first steps to find a "person of peace." Second, they would need to depend on their partners who were sent with them to identify an effective person of peace. Finally, they would have to connect with the relationships and communities of the people they found to cultivate to develop new communities of reproducing disciples. In all of the synoptic Gospels this strategy is the central focus that Jesus used for cultivating a starfish movement. Each account is recorded in Matthew 10:7–12, Mark 6:7–11, and Luke 9:1–8.

The strategy to develop the "person of peace" doesn't stop with Jesus. The apostle Paul embraced this principle and it became the building block of the starfish movement throughout the New Testament.

In Scripture, Jesus didn't say the goal was for disciples to convert the "person of peace" to Christianity, nor were they to invite them to attend a church service or a Christian event. There wasn't a focus on teaching information from the Scripture. Jesus sent them out with the power of the Holy Spirit, instructing them to share with those people who were open to hearing their stories of life change. If the person they encountered was open and responsive, they were to keep developing them to initiate a starfish movement.

Each pair that was sent out returned with the "person of peace" plus about nine others. The Scripture records that seventy-two disciples came from this exercise.

The genesis of a movement begins with the first follower.

When we talk discipleship, our process doesn't match the process from Scripture. Most of the things we do in the name of discipleship are designed to remove disciples from their pre-Christian friends and past culture. Often the goal is to teach them how to become a church person. The discipleship process most of us use is not designed to keep the new convert engaged in their pre-Christian community.

Many times new disciples exchange their pre-Christian pasts and previous friendships for new relationships with Christian friends. This process separates the new disciples from their past cultures and relationships and produces disciples who seldom ever make much of an impact on the world. This is the single-most detrimental element to launching a starfish movement.

Jesus sent His followers into the nearby relationship-rich environments of the surrounding towns. That assignment taught disciples how to depend on the Holy Spirit for their life essentials and how to find the right person to invest in. Jesus wanted to keep them focused on the Holy Spirit and the mission.

As Jesus sends the 12 out in pairs, Matthew 11:1 says, "Jesus had finished instructing his 12 disciples,…" However, there are 28 chapters in the book of Matthew. Jesus sent His disciples on their two-by-two missions relatively early in the process. He spent very little time with them providing formal instruction; instead, He sent them out with a mission. These followers were given a glimpse into the front room of the Kingdom of God. They were taught how to have spiritual conversations. He modeled for them the skill of asking important questions.

Jesus invested no time in teaching them deep theological concepts. He didn't spend time exegeting passages from Scripture, or breaking down the text for a verse-by-verse study. Jesus didn't assign His disciples to emphasize behavior modification. They were not assigned to enforce a morality code. Being a follower of Jesus was not behavior driven. As Jesus prepared His disciples, He spent no time doing what most of us would call discipleship, yet the passage says He had finished instructing them.

When the disciples returned, Jesus knew that the starfish movement was underway. He joyfully announced that Satan had fallen

(Luke 10:18–20). This was the central strategy for launching the starfish movement. If you examine the book of Acts you will discover that this same pattern continues as the central strategy for advancing the movement.

In this book we will share how this movement can begin to take shape in our lives in the US. The starfish movement is still the strategy for believers to follow. Join us on the journey

STARFISH

PART ONE

Leadership That Launches A Movement

CHAPTER 1

AT A CROSSROAD

The church as we know it is at a crossroad. Futurist writers such as Alvin Toffler have said for years that the speed at which things change is moving ever faster. We are seeing it among what is called the Millennial generation, or what I call "the flip-flop generation." A recent nationwide study revealed that just 15 percent of Millennials are involved in a local church. Nearly four out of ten consider themselves non-Christian.

That is a radical shift from the previous generation in which more than eight out of ten Gen-Xers claim to be Christian. Most of them have had a church experience at some time in their life. [4]

---

[4] Patheos research.com, January 2014.

This is a radical spiritual shift in one generation. The current generation of rising adults is different from any we have seen. Many will walk away from the church as we know it, if they are not introduced to the real person of Jesus and the movement He launched. For the most part, current and future generations will not accept or maintain the church as it is in Version 2.0.

> "Learning to do what Jesus did, is very different from learning what Jesus said…"   Alan Hirsch

Will we be a part of the Jesus movement or will we miss it? If you want to be involved in the most significant movement ever launched, learn to do the very thing in which Jesus invested His life. He invites you on a journey to explore a new way of living. In this process we will join Him in reproducing disciples who live authentic, transformed lives.

THE ADVENTURE CONTINUES

When I read about the early apostles in the book of Acts, I almost feel like I'm reading a high-adventure novel. The experiences of the early church heroes were fresh and raw. They had no expectation of what was coming, and God kept showing up to deliver them out of difficult and dangerous situations. On each page another situation arises and another amazing adventure unfolds. Time and again after reading the bold stories in Acts I my eyes fall on the everyday items in my room and I'm suddenly jerked back to reality.

I assume we all have longed to be part of a movement that looks like the courageous, scary, beautiful and faithful actions we read about in Acts. For me it grew from an obsessive curiosity into my life's calling. I am increasingly dissatisfied with anything less than what I see in the story of the early church. This pursuit has led me to arrive at something that looks like the genesis of the early church experience.

One thing I discovered early in this adventure: This movement cannot be found studying the models of growing, successful US churches, or by attending seminars or conferences. The single, most essential ingredient necessary for a starfish movement is found in the work of the Holy Spirit in each genuinely converted follower of Christ. It's inside of you; it's inside of me. It's been in us all along because each Christ follower has received His Spirit.

Alan Hirsch says, "If all the Christians in the world were suddenly killed off or abducted by aliens, and only one little Christian girl was left behind, she would have all that is necessary for God to start the entire Christian movement from her alone."[5]

The power of the kingdom of God is in Christ who is present within us. It is that simple, and yet that profound. When we complicate discipleship we ruin the amazing simple beauty inherent in the gospel.

---

[5] Hirsch, A. *The Forgotten Ways*, Grand Rapids, Mich. Brazos Press, 2006, p 19.

God has certainly empowered some to start movements. In every case, though, it is Christ who builds His church. If He is in each of us, then the seed of a massive and spontaneous expansion of His kingdom is within each of us. It is Christ who gives those very gifts to His church (Eph. 4:9–11). Never lose sight of this.

The impulse of a movement is inherent in the kingdom of God itself. You cannot manipulate the impulse. You must simply release it within yourself to allow it to flourish. We must restore our confidence in the One who placed this kingdom movement inside us, rather than in our own strategies and mechanisms. I don't remember a single time Jesus criticized His disciples because they were lacking in tactical expertise.

Today, need do not need more strategy. We need to get to know the discipleship ways of the One who first called us on this journey.

Have I Been Following Yoda and John Maxwell Instead of Jesus?

In the past, I read leadership books in the hope that someone would suggest some new, creative, imaginative and insightful formula to instruct and inspire my next step. I was on a desperate search for a leader to model. I liked Yoda, but *no books had he written.* So, I began to search for mentors who occupied this terrestrial body. I asked John Maxwell to meet with me because *many books has he written.* This was at the time I was preparing to plant my first church. John was a local pastor in San Diego, just down the road from me. He was kind, encouraging and patient with all my questions about how to start a movement.

He was honest and told me he was currently feeling the pressure to raise large sums of capital for a major church relocation project. He admitted that as much as he wanted to think about movements he didn't have the bandwidth for that topic. I appreciated his candor and patience. I learned much from his leadership, wisdom and coaching, but nothing about how to launch a movement.

John's writing and conference speaking has impacted the leadership capacities of most pastors I know. The contributions of men like John Maxwell, Bill Hybels, and Rick Warren have been largely responsible for the renewed focus on church leadership over the past 25 years . I appreciate how these men have dedicated time and energy to assist the church in making great advancements. However, in spite of all their efforts, most pastors still are deficient in leadership skills.

I say that because I recognized it my own results. The more I focused on building my leadership skills, the better the church operated. The more I grew as a directional leader, the more efficiently things ran. There still seemed to be something big missing. A smooth-running machine should not be the goal for a congregation of Christ followers.

The shiny, perpetual-motion pendulum clock on my desk ran smoothly. It had five balls suspended from a bar. The end balls smacked the stationary three, which caused the end ball on the opposite side to shoot out. This machine could hypnotize me for hours. It was a haunting illustration of the treadmill I was on. This machine worked efficiently, but it had little purpose.

> *As of late, Church leaders have been focusing on learning to lead better. Perhaps we should learn to follow Jesus better.*

I had a lot of leadership motion in my life, but what was it all for? I was becoming a better Christian leader, but why did I feel so empty? I had little satisfaction in the rapid growth of the church I led. Our systems were running smoothly. People were telling me that my leadership was improving. It seemed so hollow, what was the point?

I wanted to be a part of the movement that Jesus launched. Somehow it felt like I was disconnected from what I read in the book of Acts. The leaders in Acts seemed to have a different kind of leadership. Theirs was a discipling leadership that produced real-life change.

It seemed many of the current pastoral leaders I knew were developing directional leadership instead of discipling leadership. No one was discussing how to develop discipling leadership. Conversation about discipleship centered on how to educate people who were already convinced.

When I looked to Jesus I saw that he focused on developing discipling leadership rather than on the directional leadership that consumes the energies of most Christian leaders.

Directional leadership is the ability to mobilize people and cast an inspiring vision. These leaders often are gifted communicators. They are magnetic and can challenge others to make great sacrifices. They inspire followers to gather around a God-focused institutional church mission. They can mobilize people to step up to new challenges. These leaders can accomplish great things, and God has used them in great ways, but something still seems to be missing.

Two Kinds of Leadership

I was driving by myself on a moonless night on the Mojave Desert to meet some friends for snowboarding on Mammoth Mountain the next day. Sitting behind the wheel for six long hours, I began to reflect on the direction my life and ministry had taken. I realized I had focused solely on developing my directional leadership for most of my career.

That night I had a leadership awakening of sorts. It was as if the Holy Spirit revealed to me that I had devoted my whole focus on a small part of my leadership life. I had neglected the most important leadership area as a pastor: developing discipling leaders. I had a myopic focus on directional leadership. The pressure of leading a growing church had deceived me into thinking that solving my directional leadership issues was all I needed.

From that night on I began to shift my focus toward intentionally cultivating the discipling side of the leadership equation. No one had explained to me that there were different types of leadership development. Directional leadership is not necessarily a form of spiritual leadership. This is why pastors like John Maxwell can sell thousands of books on leadership to people who have no interest in spiritual things. Good directional leadership can be applied to any area of life and it will produce results.

Jesus was an amazing leader. He set the starfish-culture in motion. He is the focus of the movement, but He did require His physical presence or that would have bottlenecked the movement. The personal coaching I received from pastors who had created a powerful church operation focused too heavily on the directional-leadership style. I heard them say I should retain absolute control because I was the leader. Much of that logic fed my runaway desire to lead something that was significant and influential.

I followed leaders that modeled that style. Their mantras warned me "don't let the inmates run the prison. In the same way, volunteers don't get to run the church." I didn't see the connection between the church and prison, but I heard them loud and clear. If you want to lead a successful church, don't give influence to lay leaders or elder boards because it will always come back to bite you. Retain control. These leaders were so busy holding onto directional leadership that they were not training and releasing discipling leaders to change the world.

I'm not suggesting that we ignore the directional leadership needs in our churches. We simply need to develop an area we've neglected: becoming discipling leaders. Broad is the road that leads to directional leadership, but narrow is the road that leads to discipling leadership. Few leaders find the proper mix.

To be honest, I was driven by my own need to lead a high-impact ministry that would change people's lives. That sounds noble and biblical, but in my case, it was just self-serving. There is a fine line between being used as the catalyst for a movement and becoming an obstacle to the work of the Holy Spirit. I had become the major obstacle to a starfish movement.

Directional leadership impacts a congregation. Discipling leadership changes the world.

Max Lucado tells of the time he worked at a wax museum. His job was to stand to the side of the display and provide the narrative while the patrons looked at the scene. Max admitted the longer he did the job the more he immersed himself into it.

One day he found himself in the middle of the scene describing everything in great detail. He noticed people kept craning their necks to see the wax figures. He thought that he was doing his job. He realized he was keeping people from the very thing they came to see. Like Max, I had become an obstacle to the fluid work of God, standing in front of what God wanted people to see. He will use individuals as catalysts if they will model Jesus.[6]

Much of the current church culture has come from creating a directional leadership style. It says a layperson's highest level of leadership is serving on a church-governance board. This model relegates non-paid church leaders to passive attenders. This is not what a person who has been radically changed by the Spirit of Christ wants.

When most church attenders started their Christian journey, they were like you and me: they expected to live out the lives modeled in the New Testament. Most Christians get the message soon enough: Your job is to serve, attend, and tithe. Maybe the prison image is not so far-fetched after all.

Have We Become Businessmen?

At a training event for pastors in India, a national leader named Rahjal summed up directional leadership for me. He said, "Most American pastors remind me of businessmen far more than holy men." He was saying that we have mastered the skills associated with directional leadership. He saw that many of us have an underdeveloped quality of spiritual leadership.

The starfish movement isn't a missing gear in the directional leadership transmission. It is a different kind of drive train. It is the kind of leadership Jesus dedicated three years of His life to

---

[6] Max Lucado, featured speaker Saddleback Worship Conference, May 2004.

model. When Jesus launched His starfish movement, He invited many to drop what they were doing and follow him. He used His directional leadership to influence the crowds and gather a group of individuals who would follow Him. From that group He considered their behaviors as He looked for apostolic leaders who fit His criteria.

Jesus primarily taught His disciples about the Kingdom of God, and how to develop their discipling skills.

Luke 6:13 records how this unfolded: "He called His disciples to Him and chose twelve of them, whom He also designated apostles...." Jesus gathered a large group of disciples from which He identified twelve directional leaders. He assembled this group to teach them what it meant to be a part of the kingdom of God, and then to send them out to launch the starfish movement.

Jesus knew that the movement would be built on a collection of trained directional leaders. He spent approximately 18 months teaching them the principles of the new kingdom and how to multiply disciples. It is probably safe to say that these men never had anyone invest in them like Jesus did. Neither have we. Jesus masterfully cultivated their directional leadership skills while teaching them how to be discipling leaders.

Discipling Leadership is what's Missing

Our current church culture isn't developing discipling leadership. We must if we are to cultivate a starfish movement.

Mike Breen does a good job of describing this type of spiritual leadership in his book *Multiplying Missional Leaders*. He discusses the need to develop effective multiplying leaders. He suggests that a hundred years from now many books will be written on the current US church. He said, "I am fairly certain that it will be with a large degree of amazement and laughter that people, in reading about it, will say to each other, 'You must be joking! Seriously? People actually thought it was a good idea to structure the church as if it were a business?'"

Every Leader creates culture, even if it is unintentional. The question is. "Do we like the culture we have created?"

In our current leadership culture, we're expanding church campuses, but we aren't really expanding the kingdom. We are running the church machine, but we're not making kingdom impact beyond our extraordinarily well-run Christian playgrounds.[7]

Churches rarely focus on discipling leadership qualities. Instead, their urgent need for volunteers to run the programs drives the

---

[7] Mike Breen, *Multiplying Missional Leaders*, 3DM Publishing, Pawleys Island, SC, 2012. p.5.

churchification of all new converts and attenders. The desperate volunteer need in many churches requires everyone to roll up his or her sleeves and become a loyal worker.

Jesus was never in a desperate panic to find leaders who would enlist volunteers. Jesus perfectly blended the cultivation of both leadership styles in His twelve disciples. Much of the focus over the past 30 years has been to paint Jesus as a type-A, driven, directional leader. It doesn't help that most of the current leadership writings describe Jesus as a CEO-type of leader—Laurie Beth Jones' *Jesus CEO;* Ken Blanchard's *Lead Like Jesus;* and many others—and focus on the directional aspects of Jesus' leadership style. Such authors portray Jesus as a directional leader. However, His primary focus with the twelve was to cultivate discipling world changers.

You Can Teach Discipling Leadership, but Not Directional Leadership

Jesus proved directional leaders can be taught how to become discipling leaders, but it's impossible to teach directional/apostolic leadership. It can be developed in a person, but that person must have the core elements of a leader. God has either gifted you with the capacity for directional/apostolic leadership or He has another plan for you. This is the reason He selected twelve men who were already directional/apostolic leaders. With the empowering help of the indwelling Holy Spirit, a starfish movement can be launched.

The Johari window below, helps to illustrate four current leadership types. They are the anthill leader, tombstone leader, house-church leader, and starfish leader

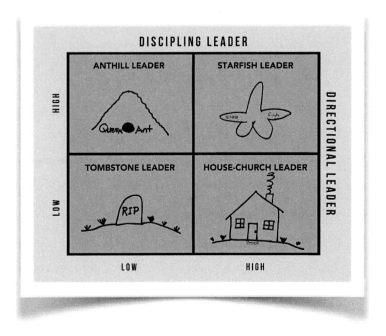

When a directional leader learns the skills necessary to become a discipling leader he or she moves into the category of the starfish leader. The directional versus discipling leadership principle is similar to the one in the parable of the soils. Jesus explains that three of the four soil types produce nothing, like in the above illustration. Three of the four leadership-style combinations will be minimally effective at launching a multiplication movement. They can be effective at discipling individuals, but not in launching a movement. To launch a movement that reproduces disciples requires a directional/apostolic leader to learn how to apply the core principles of discipleship multiplication.

The two leadership styles that have high directional leadership are on top. They are the anthill leader and the starfish leader. Most growing U.S. churches have a strong, highly directional but low discipling leader. This is the anthill leader. In most cases this leader has adopted a CEO corporate version of church leadership. These leaders can create a well-run church.

> *The church is known for it's affection for institutions and programs. It should be known for a passion to make disciples who make disciples.*

On the lower right-hand side we have a leader who is focused on discipling others, but who seldom leads a movement or reproduces other leaders to do what he or she knows how to do. This is a house-church leader. This leader strongly invests in one person at a time. He or she is usually a teacher who wants to transfer information to a student. Churches that have an organic flavor can do great things, but it is hard for much momentum ever to be realized.

Most house churches lack directional leadership. Rarely can other people connect with a scattered group of individuals who do their own thing.

Unfortunately, a house church is seldom led with a clear vision because it lacks a compelling leadership concept to unite them.

These groups gather under the banner of what they don't want to be. In many cases a house church comes together because of a felt need Christians have for fellowship and community.

Regrettably, the tombstone leaders are low in both leadership areas. They aren't directional and they have never been taught discipling skills. We have an abundance of this leadership style in US churches. Many pastors are teachers who love to transmit the truth of Scripture, but they lack natural directional-leadership qualities. Therefore, they haven't developed discipleship-reproduction abilities.

In Jesus' illustration of the soils, He established that all four types have a potential season of growth. All four require the same effort to sow seeds. However, even though the effort is the same, the results are radically different.

All healthy living things reproduce.
How healthy is your church?

In Jesus' parable, the one soil with the right combination produced thirty, sixty, and hundredfold. That translates to 3,000, 6,000, and 10,000 percent growth. Stories from the New Testament remind us that its necessary to combine the power of the directional/apostolic leadership qualities with the discipling leadership skills that Jesus revealed. When those abilities are combined with the work of the Holy Spirit, the result is a starfish movement

CHAPTER 2

HOW DO WE MAKE AN IMPACT?

A man once counseled his son that if he wanted to make an impact, the secret was to sprinkle a little gunpowder on his oatmeal every morning. So the trusting son never missed a morning without his oatmeal and gunpowder. The boy lived to the ripe old age of 93. When he died, he left four children, 20 grandchildren, 35 great-grandchildren, and a 15-foot hole in the wall of the crematorium. That is impact! 8

We want to make an impact as spiritual leaders. It doesn't matter how deeply we desire to launch a starfish-multiplication culture,

---

8 longislandfirearms.com

God uses a certain type of leader. In the New Testament we see lives changed by the thousands by people who came long after the apostles were gone. If a leader has low-directional leadership and low-discipling leadership skills he or she will be a tombstone leader. He or she will not be able to mobilize a group of people to make the radical shift necessary to initiate a starfish disciple-making culture.

I'm describing this kind of leader because many good leaders want to see the "valley of dry bones" (Ezekiel 37) come to life. God tends to use an apostolic leader to do this work. Apostolic leaders often have a relatively brief season in one place. They can become restless and are soon ready to move on.

Anthill Leaders

A few years ago I moved to a beach town in South Carolina. This thriving coastal area had about 100 golf courses. We bought a house on one of them and every spring we watched an odd ritual begin. The greens keepers would apply an insecticide that would run bothersome fire ants off the fairway – and into the neighboring yards along the course.

Because I had previously spent most of my time on the Pacific coast I knew nothing about these ferocious little critters. I had no idea I was dealing with miniature terrorists. These varmints pinch you with their tiny legs and inject venom that will make your appendage swell up and burn red hot. I was shocked such a little insect could create such a vicious wound.

I went to the local Home Depot and bought several bags of chemicals to fight fire with fire. I eventually learned you cannot kill fire ants, you can only do what the golf course did – drive them to the neighbor's. So being the kind, loving Christian I am, I bought my chemicals and chased them next door.

Like most ants they work in colonies and create anthills, which is basically the home and support network for the queen ant. One queen ant can produce up to 50,000 drone ants *each month*. The anthill can grow up to two-feet tall and stretch five feet underground.

If you step on the anthill you discover it is made mostly of air and sand particles. It knocks over easily. As soon as you kick it, thousands of ants immediately rebuild the mound. If you look closely, you will notice the primary building material is sand and the dead bodies of hundreds of thousands of ants.[9]

This is the metaphor I use to describe the leadership style modeled in most of our American churches. The lead pastor has the job of getting all of the ants to work together to make all of the complex components of the church work. It takes an amazing amount of effort to pull off a Sunday-morning event in most churches.

It made me sad to think the monument of the anthill is built with the bodies of the multitude of volunteers who have burned out and left the anthill church. Had I used them to build this monu-

---

[9]Bert Holidobler & Edward O.Wilson, *The Ants*, Antark, p48.

ment? Is this what I was called to do when I first began to follow Jesus?

As I reflected, I could see the faces of so many of them. Often they began as energized new followers of Jesus. They were hoping we would help them find a new life purpose. In many cases we led them to pray and pray, we baptized them and simply signed them up to be volunteers and join a small group. We tried to love them, encourage them, and develop them.

I noticed many of them weren't with us anymore. Where did they go? We had such a steady stream of new attenders it seemed like we didn't need to stop and reflect on what happened to the ones who were gone. I'm sure several of them ended up disillusioned with the process. We had built an anthill on the bodies of those who had hoped they would find more than a programmed machine. I wonder if they had been in a starfish movement if they would have had a different outcome.

The Directional Anthill Leader

Churches that grow rapidly in America usually do so under an effective directional leader. Directional leaders are able to gather church attenders who are glad to be in a vibrant environment with good worship and where Scripture is taught. But, when the directional leadership overshadows the discipling aspect, you tend to get an anthill church.

Today, we define leadership differently than they did in the New Testament. The leadership style we celebrate is that of CEO. The kind of gifted leaders that are growing American churches today could apply their skills in any number of corporate settings and do very well. That is not to say they aren't led by God and aren't genuine and sincere. It just means the type of leader who is leading growing churches is a high-caliber leader.

These are leaders who almost always have high directional leadership skills. I believe God gives an apostolic gift to these leaders. Having said that, many of them have been deliberate to cultivate their directional leadership qualities. They almost never develop a culture of discipleship multiplication.

> *Churches have developed an institutional language rather than a discipling language.*

At first glance it can appear these churches are a movement, but most of the time they are effective attractional churches. They attract people who are inclined toward church attendance. It is possible for the anthill leader to put together the right combination of attractional components. The result can be such a rapid addition of attenders coming through the doors that it looks like multiplication.

The missing piece in an anthill church is the rapid discipleship multiplication culture that Jesus launched. Many anthill churches claim to be discipleship churches, but the ministry fruit produced from the anthill is seldom multiplication. Often the anthill leaders are invested in such a way they are personally connected to every significant decision. These leaders may have a delegation style as it relates to tasks, but everyone in the anthill church is on a short leash.

The above description is primarily leaders who work through paid staff to direct the operation. Leaders who are in smaller churches, or who are church planters, often have studied and imitated this leadership style. In either case, they still think and act in the category of the anthill leader—hoping someday they will lead a mega anthill church.

Ant Abuse

I've had the privilege of leading two large churches that reached an attendance of anthill proportion. At the time, it seemed to be what was necessary to accomplish the lofty goals I had set. I was convinced these goals were from God and they were certainly going to advance His Kingdom. The volunteers were friends, many of whom I had led to Christ.

But, I have a confession to make. I was guilty of treating volunteers like drone ants. I expected that after they came to Christ they would be faithful servants who would help me build the anthill monument. And I called this process discipleship. I taught them that serving in the anthill was their highest purpose in the kingdom of God.

We took great pride in treating our new converts well. We recruited them to volunteer, and we trained them to do their tasks well. We encouraged them, loved them, and celebrated their efforts. Everything seemed to work. The volunteers did a great job, they gave sacrificially, and we kept building the anthill. We couldn't ask for more from the volunteers—they were amazing. They tithed their money, their time, and their energy. However, I finally recognized they were going from being new converts to being volunteers without being disciples.

I had to repent of viewing these Christ followers as ants to build the anthill. At first, most of the new converts appreciated the simplicity of being included in the church without having overwhelming responsibilities.

It all seemed to work. I was growing as a leader. The anthill kept growing. Why did it not satisfy? Was I making a mountain out of my anthill? The distressing part for me was that my experience was not matching the picture of the New Testament church in the book of Acts.

In the New Testament, new converts were not given a simple reproducible task and treated as a drone ant. Instead, they were treated as valued leaders. They were quickly developed into communities that established new churches. They shared boldly what God had done in their lives. They became life changers and then world changers. The picture between what I was reading in Acts and what I was leading didn't match up.

Where did this church culture I had embraced come from? I began to question some older leaders. One, who lived to be 108, explained the church volunteer culture we know hasn't always been around. It emerged during the Industrial Revolution of a century ago.

It was a time that produced the assembly line. Manufacturers learned how to break down the production of goods into tiny tasks that could be done by low-paid, low-trained workers. The business community discovered that if these employees would do their jobs on an assembly line, products could be produced cheaply and efficiently.

The church discovered that if it could create a factory environment where attenders could participate in a franchised system, then the church could ensure a consistent product in every town across America. This period ushered in the rise of franchised denominational churches. This model flourished from the 1930s to the 1980s.

This picture describes the traditional anthill church that many of our parents and grandparents attended. The current contemporary church has fallen into the same anthill snare that captured our parents' and grandparents' churches. We have continued to cultivate the Industrial Revolution, programmed church model in the contemporary church. The only thing that has changed is the worship style. The current anthill church has franchised campuses and video venues as a more current version of the anthill Industrial Revolution church.

I have been the founding pastor of multi-site churches and the kind of church I just described. This is not intended to be a criticism of the programmed anthill church, rather, a review of how we got here. We can move from where we are now to a movement of starfish churches.

In the New Testament, we don't see followers being reduced to mere cogs on an assembly line. Jesus did not die on the cross so a vibrant follower could serve on a committee until he learned enough biblical information to serve on the elder board and reach the pinnacle of spiritual life.

> *We were created to make an eternal impact with our lives. When we fall short of that reality, we end up feeling hollow and empty inside.*

The tombstone committee and board structure is another function of the Industrial Revolution church. It looks a lot more like a political/corporate model than something Jesus launched. The anthill is not much different. They changed the working words "committee" and "board" to the word "team" but there is not much difference. Teams are more casual and more action focused, but they still miss what Jesus intended – discipled followers who are fully empowered to engage in amazing kingdom advancement.

In fact, Jesus said in John 14:12, "And you will do even greater things than these... (than I have done)." This idea is at the heart of the starfish movement. The Apostle Paul, in Ephesians 4:11, explains some were designed to "be apostles, some prophets, some evangelists, some pastors and teachers, for the training of the saints in the work of ministry..."

Evangelism Anthills

In the anthill church it's not uncommon to have a high focus on evangelism. I had to admit my focus on evangelism was not for making disciples. My focus was directed toward having new converts be faithful to the mission of serving in the anthill, inviting new people to the anthill, and sacrificing for the anthill. I had made volunteering in the church synonymous to serving God and advancing the Kingdom. Upon further reflection, many of the faithful ants who had gone before them were literally the foundation on which we had built the monument.

The Unintended Consequences of the Anthill

God has definitely used anthill leaders in significant ways. They have developed their directional/apostolic gifting and have grown large churches. Most anthill leaders I know are loved by their congregations.

However, I notice several trends. In many cases, the larger the anthill church, the more rapid the turnover rate of its pastoral staff. This is especially true among Baby Boomer mega-church anthill pastors. Most anthill leaders tend to hire leaders from other churches who have a high level of skill, in contrast to the starfish leader who develops leaders from within the culture.

When this happens it is usually accompanied by long years of relationship, even when the leader leaves to launch a new church.

It is not uncommon for the anthill leaders to create work environments that have excessive expectations and an unreasonable work pace. It seems the anthill leader's low discipling tendency weighs most on his staff culture more than on anyone else. The lack of staff discipleship development wears on staff leaders. I find many pastoral staff stay a few of years and then move on, often leaving exhausted and discouraged.

We are in a season unique to our time. When I was born, there were very few mega anthill churches. Forty years ago there were only a handful. At the same time, every community had many churches that were vibrant and alive. Today, every city has a number of large mega anthill churches; however, if you look at the outlying areas you will find those formerly alive churches are dying. There is a reason the mega anthill church in America is exploding. People are gathering around the last vestige of what appears to be a vibrant church.

I watched the same thing occur as my parents died. The doctor warned us their hands and feet would begin to turn blue and appear lifeless. Their mid-sections began to swell and become warm. The doctor explained they were in the final stages of life. He explained when the human body begins to die it will often try to rally one last time. This is the body's last ditch effort to save itself. It will pull all the resources from the outer appendages of the body and send everything it has to the vital organs.

The result is the hands and feet become icy cold. The mid-section swells because of the extra blood sent to that area. If you didn't know better you could assume dad is doing better. He is bulging in the mid-section. Does that mean he is growing again? The truth is stark.

The same thing is happening to the local church. The once vibrant smaller churches are now all but empty. Meanwhile, the churches in the population centers are drawing attenders from the outlying appendage churches. The growth of the mega church is not a positive sign. It is the sign of a radically different future for the church in the US.

House-Church Leaders

Many international house churches are vibrant starfish communities that reproduce disciples. If they are a starfish movement, there is usually an apostolic/directional leader who has put a reproductive, biblically focused culture in place. This leader is the one who cast an apostolic vision and has influenced the training and coaching culture. Most starfish movements use the home setting for their meetings, especially in the early stages.

The organizer of a house church may have the ability to gather a group under a single idea. But if he or she lacks leadership the group may well go off in a number of unfocused directions that have no continuity.

It is not uncommon for such a group to have broken off from an anthill church. This type of group may be strong at learning scriptures, but will never multiply disciples. In this case the absence of apostolic/directional leadership mixed with the wrong type of discipling leadership produces a house church or single cell group that doesn't last more than a couple of years. These groups may have a love for each other but will languish under the lack of directional leadership.

They also tend to become inwardly focused. This ingrown perspective will result in a short shelf life. This group will seldom grow beyond the size of a single cell.

Often this leader has a teaching gift but beyond that, not much leadership influence. Teaching and leadership gifts are not interchangeable.

Often house church leaders react to the anthill leadership style. They often can forge a group of people who have a trauma bond, uniting around a church leadership conflict. The two groups that most contribute to this occurrence come from the leadership style of the tombstone or the anthill leader.

A group that is bonded together due to trauma becomes unified by its agreement on what's wrong with the anthill or the tombstone church. Members convince themselves that directional leadership is what is wrong with the church at large. As a result, they create an environment that eliminates the directional leader.

These groups often form around what they are against. They lack a vision informed by the Great Commission of Jesus. If they are established by a negative vision, they will not last long.

New churches are often birthed out of a reaction to an existing negative church environment.

Generally groups form "for or against" in response to directional leadership. Like it or not, God uses directional leaders. The New Testament church was shaped through directional leaders. These leaders led the discipleship reproduction process through the power of the Holy Spirit. In both the New Testament and Old Testament, God uses directional leaders to lead His church.

TOMBSTONE LEADERS

All leaders have a place in the starfish movement. A leader who doesn't possess the qualities of a directional or apostolic leader will still have a vital role as the starfish movement develops.

The tombstone leader simply lacks both directional and discipling leadership skills. This leader cannot mobilize the critical components required to launch a movement. Don't feel bad about it. You still have skills and there's a place for you, just not as the pioneer to launch the movement.

The tombstone is not associated with a worship style; it's also not a code word for traditional churches. Interestingly, churches of every worship style regularly select leaders who don't have the ability to lead a movement. The tombstone emerges when there is an absence of leadership.

This absence creates the dying church.

Churches must be lead by leaders.

There are many reasons why churches appoint pastors with virtually no leadership ability. Sometimes churches don't realize they have chosen such a leader until they see the church on a plateau or spiraling toward death.

Often these churches embrace a stealth-leadership culture that undermines the lead pastors. Committee-based churches are often designed to keep anyone from truly leading. Stealth leadership can happen when a dominant family has taken control and insists on a nepotism-leadership culture. This phase can occur when a church adopts a highly bureaucratic style of governance.

It was recognition of the high number of tombstone churches during the 2000s that motivated a focus on leaderships. Despite the efforts to strengthen leadership in the local church, this is still the largest category of leaders today.

The tombstone leaders are not doomed. There really aren't tombstone "leaders." These individuals are persons misplaced in the lead role who need to find their appropriate place in the movement. They need to allow directional leaders to fill the leadership role. The essential element of apostolic leadership is missing. As much as they want to, they can't and won't launch a movement.

> *Leadership most always emerges from a leader… leadership seldom emerges from a committee.*

I will discuss later how God uses all types of leaders to make disciples. I have found that tombstone leaders can be some of the most significant leaders once the starfish movement has started.

In many cases, mainline congregations have built a culture that is leadership resistant. These churches trusted the denominations of the past to lead them programmatically. This occurred during the industrial-revolution phase of church development. They became program churches.

Sometimes these churches have built a leadership-resistant environment and no one will ever be able to lead them. The culture is so ingrained that they seek only tombstone leaders to be their pastors. This leadership resistance is one of the primary elements that led them to a state of decline and death.

> *Leadership resistant cultures are seldom aware that they have become impossible to lead.*

The tombstone, anthill, and house-church models constrain the leadership possibilities of its participants. When Jesus launched the starfish movement it was designed to release the amazing leadership capacities of all Christ followers. If you want to release a starfish movement in your setting, you must unlearn what you know about leadership and church structure.

STARFISH LEADERS

Starfish leaders – like anthill leaders – have high directional leadership qualities. The difference is that they have developed their discipling leadership potential. Jesus knew it takes a directional and a discipling leader to create a starfish movement. A directional leader Himself, He selected directional leaders to be His disciples. He assigned His 12 leaders to select other directional leaders. He told His disciples to find these leaders whom

He called "persons of peace." He told them to invest all their time in them, sharing the discipleship leadership principles He had given them. The key was to discover and develop leaders who would reproduce disciples.

We are leading like Jesus when we invest in disciples who will multiply other disciples.

As I examined how Jesus made disciples, I also evaluated my own leadership style and realized I had neglected to develop my discipling leadership skill. I had spent years attending two seminaries. I had attended conferences and read shelves of books on leadership. I had started several businesses in my teens and early twenties. I had overdeveloped my directional leadership, but I had neglected my discipling leadership skill. I had missed the very thing that was essential to launching a disciple-making movement.

The real question is: Where do I go to learn how to be a discipling leader? This leadership skill is best learned by transmission in a local starfish environment. It is virtually impossible to learn this skill in an institutional setting. I could not find anyone who could teach me how to build the skill of discipling leadership. So, I decided to use Jesus as my model and ruthlessly followed His example.

I poured over how He did everything. I did not want to assume my cultural Christian/church bias was biblical. I asked the Holy

Spirit to lead me as I began to find a group of disciple-able "persons of peace." I allowed this group of Spirit-led individuals to walk with me through the learning process of how to launch a starfish movement. I soon realized I had to eliminate much of the ministry clutter from my life to create the space for real starfish discipling to take place. This was something I hadn't been willing to do in the past.

Starfish

CHAPTER 3

THE MISGUIDED PAWN
THE DISTRACTED KING

We can learn a lot about disciple making through the lives of two chess pieces — the king and the pawn. I had to decide which I was going to be. My identity was always a type-A driven achiever. I had been the hard working pawn — expendable but useful and admired. Let me explain.

Let's say the pawn is hanging out on the shelf and he overhears the other pieces talking. The pawn knows his abilities and limits. He understands his role on the game board. He can move one space at a time in a forward direction. He embraces that. The pawn's dilemma is that he doesn't see the overall objective of the game.

Now, on the shelf, the pawn built a relationship with the game piece from checkers. The checker reminds him the goal is to work hard, get to the end of the board and be crowned king. So the next time the pawn is on the game board, he spends all his energies pushing toward the same goal as the checkers piece. The problem is, he's playing by the wrong rules.

The rules of chess and checkers differ. The board looks the same, the pawn and the checker are both front line game pieces, but they are radically different.

THE MISGUIDED PAWN

The pawn has been discipled with the wrong information. Many pastoral leaders are in the same place. Maybe they came from a marketplace career and transfer market principles directly into the world of ministry. This is the single greatest contributor for why the church has embraced a business CEO model for ministry. So, it makes sense that church leaders adopt an anthill style of leadership. It is common for a church leader to begin as a hard-working, focused church attender/volunteer and eventually become a directional pastoral leader. Many pastors who are skilled as directional leaders have watched other leaders display their directional skill and assume the key to growing their congregations is to work hard as a directional leader, get to the end of the board and be crowned king.

It is common for a directional leader to transfer business principles to ministry – hard work and even motivational thinking. The planter and his family frequently make great personal sacrifices in the name of ministry. It is not uncommon for new pastors to embrace almost every ministry opportunity that comes along. These qualities are not bad, they just produce an exhausted leader.

> *Pastors who blindly engage in every opportunity that comes along, tend to be leaders who operate out of a compulsive, fear, instead of a godly conviction.*

Launching a life-changing culture will never emerge from hard work alone. It is not possible to focus yourself into a starfish movement with motivational thinking. This leader has embraced the focused but confused pawn syndrome. That is the mistaken belief that the harder I work the sooner I'll become king (the successful leader I want to be).

A leader will not be effective if he has embraced the wrong objective. Jesus calls us to make disciples, not to transfer business practices into the church so it will grow into an anthill.

THE DISTRACTED KING

Everyone knows security of the king is priority number one in chess. Without him the game is over. Despite his lofty importance the king's mobility is much like the pawn's. He can only move one space at a time. Mobility and value are very different. The king has limited mobility, but high value.

Good chess players know how to accentuate the strength of the king and minimize his weakness. It is best if the king doesn't move much at all. The more he moves the more he is exposed and the more everything is at risk. The directional leader is much the same. The more distracted and busier he or she is, the more the starfish culture is at risk. Directional leaders have to fight the temptation to fall back into pawn-like confusion.

They must remember checkers and chess may have the same playing surface, but they are very different. It's the same thing for the leader coming from a business culture who assumes the playing surfaces are the same between the workplace and the church.

The directional leader is primarily responsible for keeping the culture at the center of everything the church does. God has given directional leaders an essential role to play in launching a starfish culture. Without this leader, most movements never form. Directional leaders may not be any more talented or capable than those they lead. Most have dominant strengths and great weaknesses.

It is common for directional leaders to focus too much on improving their weak areas, thinking that will make them more complete leaders. A leader's weaknesses are given by God just as are strengths. Weaknesses have a purpose; they force the leader to depend on the Spirit.

If the directional leader gets distracted, the culture is at risk. The leader's main role is keeping everyone focused on the primary mission. The more distracted he becomes the more the culture is in danger of losing its focus. These leaders must fight the temptation to become bottlenecks, a narrow funnel that prevents growth.

Jesus launched a culture of leaders who would simplify and focus on one mission: to make reproducing disciples. He did not model busyness and distraction. He sent His leaders with a clear mission to follow the Holy Spirit's leading so they could accomplish that one mission. The disciples were to identify and develop a "person of peace" (Luke 10:6). If they became preoccupied and busy, they would not accomplish the one thing He commanded and commissioned them to do.

Trying to lead a church without the power of the Holy Spirit will create the greatest leadership challenge you'll ever face.

Jesus told a story of a master who gave one instruction and departed. The master made it clear his servants had one task — to reproduce what he had given them. Jesus expects us to reproduce disciples. It is the one thing He told us to do.

Jesus gave several warnings of what happens when we get distracted from our mission or hide the abilities He has given us. He calls those leaders "wicked" (Matthew 25:26). When we get busy and lose our focus it's because we have been operating with a wrong view of our purpose.

Change What You Care About

All leaders must be discipled to change what they care about, to let go of anything that competes with the commission of making disciples who will reproduce disciples.

Preferred vs. Practiced Values

Adjusting your values is at the heart of "changing what you care about." We all have a set of driving principles that guide us. They are our practiced values – what we really care about. We hardly know how we arrived at our driving set of practiced principles and values. I describe it as the invisible giant funnel attached to the top of our heads. We all have one. It's where all the variety of experiences, failures, successes and influences pour into our lives. All these things helped us arrive at what drives us.

Enron's preferred values were:
"Integrity, Honesty, Respect, Excellence."

The idea of our inner values and way of life is expressed by the Greek word *ethos*. When we encounter Jesus, we are confronted with an invitation to "change what we care about." He makes it clear if we are to follow Him we must begin to allow Him to alter our values or our *ethos*. He says things such as: "Take up your cross daily and follow me" (Luke 9:23).

Often the set of preferred values we claim differs radically from what we really believe, as expressed by our actions. When we operate in the realm of theory we can afford to claim a set of preferred values. But, when things get real, we will always operate from our practiced values.

Businesses and churches spent great amounts of time over the past 20 years fashioning proper wording of their mission statements and values. Organizations spent hours and thousands of dollars crafting a carefully worded mission statement. All the while, most were operating from a different set of practiced values. Perfectly worded statements don't alter engrained, practiced values that differ from preferred values.

This leadership generation is helping reset the values discussion. They are open to "change what they care about." For many new leaders from the Millennial generation, relationships are the first item on the agenda. Crossing the finish line is not in the equation. In fact, there is so little talk about the finish line it seems out of place.

Changing What You Care About: Theory vs. Starfish Movement

Changing what we care about is central to launching a starfish movement. We need to shift from idealistic dreaming of the past generations to focus on changing a single life in such a way that it becomes simple to repeat the process. It also must be simple enough that it's contagious. This happens best by learning how to reduce the process into bite-sized digestible parts that can be assimilated. If we continue to talk about the grand movement of the starfish idea, it all grinds to a halt. If it remains simple and manageable, it will be passed from one life to another like a happy virus. It will remain relational and contagious.

Simple is less fragile. Simple is repeatable. Simple builds confidence as it's passed to each succeeding generation of disciples.

Complex is much more stressful; complex creates bureaucracy and process. Complex creates proprietary ownership and hierarchy.

If the group looks to a single vision caster for all its direction and leadership, a bottleneck is created. This happens when every decision must pass through a narrow process for movement to occur. This process creates a dependency that crushes real multiplication.

> *Complex leadership structures were absent in the New Testament church. They remained laser focused on the mission Jesus gave them.*

Leadership in a movement isn't who sits at the top of the pyramid. It's empowering others to embrace the process, and in turn make necessary changes that will keep it building and growing until it becomes a movement.

Changing What You Care About: Building a Culture vs. Bureaucracies

You'll hear, "That's the way we've always done it before," in a bureaucratic environment, where the highest authority is the bylaws, policy, and procedural manual. As the church fossilizes, it becomes more skilled at programs that can easily function without the help of the Holy Spirit.

Institutions create policy and procedures to protect the legacy and the organization. Creating a disciple-making culture is proactive. It keeps the focus on Jesus and His commission. When the mission is the focus, the attention is outward where it belongs. When churches turn their attention inward, their goal becomes incremental improvement, which before long turns into preservation.

Incrementalism is the process of making superficial changes that never have significant impact. If we focus on competing with other churches, it reveals our desire to become incrementally better than them. Categorical change is about giving up on superficial improvements, and refocusing on a totally new way to view the world. Multiplication only happens when we see the need to make this change. This is why we talk about "changing what we care about."

We will only be able to focus on multiplying disciples when we make a categorical change. We will never incrementally arrive on our own efforts to where God wants us. Incrementalism keeps us making gradual steps along the wrong route. The goal is not to become a better American-styled version of church. Jesus came to bring us a totally new version. He did not come to improve on the Pharisees' corrupted version of religion.

> *The Kingdom of God that Jesus introduced is categorically different from anything that came before.*

Jesus came to bring a categorical shift that would require us either to embrace His Kingdom culture or reject it. He was not about incrementally producing more consumers of religious goods and services. Jesus invited His first group of disciples in the Matthew 4:15–19 passage to make a categorical change. He warned it would require them to go in a new direction, He says: "(Make a U-turn) repent and believe the good news, then come follow me...and I will make you fishers of men."

> *The Kingdom doesn't advance on incremental change.*

Jesus explains when we follow Him as a disciple we automatically make our first categorical shift. The invitation is to repent, or turn, from the old superficial way of thinking and embrace the good news and follow Him. To pursue His kingdom requires a 180-degree turn. After repenting from the old behavior that focuses on incremental worldview, it is necessary to embrace the freedom that following Jesus gives us.

Changing What You Care About: Taking Risk vs. Care Taking

Fear can quickly overtake a church, which produces an emphasis on survival. You see this when leaders talk more about cost than Christ, and more about money than mission. When a church decides not to concern itself with survival and legacy it will be empowered to take risks. Caution is the atrophy that sets in when a group focuses on pain avoidance instead of pushing the envelope. Craig Groeschel says, "To reach people that no one is reaching, you have to do things that no one is doing."

The greatest threat to a potential movement is the success that prominence draws. It tempts a leader to keep doing what draws attention and gets recognition. Before long the focus turns to retaining respect and influence. Before long, growing larger becomes the goal. It is easy to be deceived into thinking we are succeeding when we add more services, campuses, and zeros to our budget. Following Jesus always takes us toward the "least of these," far more than the most and the best. The movement in the New Testament thrived when it was in the alley, not on Main Street.

Changing What You Care About: Structure vs. Spirit

It is always a battle to make structure submit to the Spirit. Success and growth creates complexity. Before long, layers of structure and process are required to support the institution. Every added staff member creates a thirst for more processes. A vibrant movement can create its own hamster wheel of busyness and bureaucracy. It is best to flatten the organizational structure so it can remain reliable and responsive.

The Perfect Strategy for a Starfish Movement

When my wife and I lived as missionaries in Israel we saw the brilliance of Jesus' strategy as He intentionally chose where to live and who He selected as disciples. The Old Testament prophesied the Messiah would bring the illumination of the gospel to the northern region of the Sea of Galilee in Isaiah 9:1–2.

It was wonderful that Jesus intentionally selected fishermen. They were the sociological group on the lowest rung of Jewish culture, yet they had a communal lifestyle.

One group lower than fishermen on the cultural ladder was those who herded pigs and sheep. They were nomads who lived among the livestock, mostly because they had to be on the move to constantly find new grazing land for the animals. Their jobs made them social outcasts because they were associated with the animals they herded. And, their nomadic life would have made it impossible ever to gather as a group for any length of time.

Fishermen were almost as repulsive to the Jewish religious culture as animal herders. Their trade required them to catch, sort and sell the fish. A person who touched a dying animal was considered unclean. Jesus intentionally selected fishermen whose communal lifestyle would allow Jesus to reproduce a discipleship culture in a village and then in a region.

After Jesus selected the Twelve from His discipleship pool, He took them to the surrounding towns and villages, laying the foundation for the discipleship launch strategy. Within two years, this group would be sent in pairs to those same towns to launch the starfish multiplication movement we call the Church.

It's necessary to learn the process of detox if a person is going to make disciples like Jesus did. First, Jesus took the 12 apostolic leaders He selected from the group of disciple candidates and He isolated them for approximately 18 months.

He used that time to give them another way to view the world. He gave them a picture of what the Father was like as later described in John 14:9. He wanted them to think differently about everything. The isolation of the Twelve was necessary so they could see the contrast between His starfish movement and the cultural milieu the Pharisees and Sadducees embraced.

Next, Jesus gave each member of this core a chance to learn the ways of the Spirit of God. He would heal, teach and connect with common people. This season was focused on the 12 disciples learning how to function in the new Kingdom movement He was launching.

STARFISH

CHAPTER 4

DETOX IS NECESSARY

Our church culture, like the religious culture of Jesus' time, has embraced behaviors that prevent starfish multiplication. Jesus had to detox His disciples before a movement could take root. Likewise, we need to detox if we are going to launch a starfish movement.

The last few times I moved my family, it was to launch a starfish multiplication culture. With each relocation I found a group of people who embraced this new way of reproducing disciples. Carlsbad, California, and Myrtle Beach, South Carolina are coastal areas with large secular populations and only a small number of cultural Christians. They required less detox because they weren't immersed in the ways of traditional church.

I have progressively learned to identify individuals who are open to the vibrations of the Holy Spirit. Even in a secular environment some detox is necessary to move away from cultural Christian assumptions. Where we served, we found less than five percent of the people were attending church.

Bible-belt areas require more patience. It takes longer for starfish multiplication to take root, because the "church culture" works against authentic New Testament discipleship. Those who are engaged in a cultural Christian environment are often inoculated to the authentic work of the Holy Spirit that produces discipleship multiplication.

THE VIRUS

Jesus warned us we would need to deal with the virus. He told His disciples in Matthew 16:6, "Be on your guard against the yeast of the Pharisees and Sadducees." Yeast permeates everything. It changes the physical properties of bread. It is impossible to see individual yeast spore, but its impact on bread is obvious.

Pharisees and Sadducees were unaware they had been impacted by this foreign agent, and they were tools for its spread. In another passage Jesus taught that a subtle agent, called tares, had the same ability to alter a wheat crop. Jesus indicated tares were introduced by a spiritual enemy. He the Pharisees and Sadducees were the ones who were continuing to promote this destructive spiritual element in the name of God.

Think of a modern yeast as a computer virus. When I open up my computer, I never know what awaits me in the world of viruses and hackers. I have come to expect these intrusions. As with yeast, I cannot see a virus and am unaware when I have come in contact with it. My computer provides a series of warning signs about a virus or malware. The processing speed slows way down. I get unexpected interruptions, and the machine shuts down for no reason.

If I have a virus, I can do one of two things: ignore the warning signs and try to continue on as if nothing has happened, or address the problem. If I ignore the warnings, it won't be long until my laptop becomes just an ornamental piece of plastic. If I address the problem, I have a chance to restore my machine and get back to work.

Most Christians in America have been infected with the yeast of the Pharisees.

The yeast to which Jesus referred is a destructive, undetectable element that corrupts and destroys. The virus present in our churches is just as dangerous to us now as the yeast of the Pharisees and Sadducees was then. The resistance of the US church to the starfish culture is a virus.

It shows up in many different forms. The virus has affected our operating system. It has caused us to shut down the very thing Jesus told us to do. We stop the starfish multiplication process and settle for church operations. As a result, we tend to care about things for which Jesus didn't have much concern. The virus causes us to focus on buildings, budgets, attendance, to improve the attractional environment, and to count converts.

We create environments that fail to transform people, and even hinder transformation. We fall into the trap of gauging success by superficial measurements. Jesus used no such measures. During His time on earth, He owned little to nothing. The Bible even says He had no place to lay His head, much less a building for public meetings (Luke 9:58). The Son of God could have acquired a meeting space if it was important to Him. It obviously was not a priority. We must ask why it's so high on our priority list.

The American church has become excessively focused on meetings, programs, and events.

The virus distracts us into thinking of ministry as being related to public gatherings and crowds of people. Yes, Jesus did speak to the masses, but He consistently focused on coaching the Twelve. His time with the masses was to allow the Twelve to have public favor when they went in groups of two to the surrounding towns and villages.

MOST OF US HAVE NEVER
BEEN DISCIPLED

I believe most of us have never been discipled.

We've learned church culture. We've been taught how to read our Bible, tithe, and serve in the church. But growing strong as a Christ follower is about walking with and loving Jesus. When we reproduce that process in others, we grow to a new level.

The virus has changed the proper definition of discipleship and substituted a counterfeit definition that makes us think discipleship is merely one of the options in the church cafeteria. It equates Bible study and discipleship, leaving us theologically informed but with no real understanding of the commission of Jesus.

Discipleship is a way of life, not a church program or even intense Bible study. The term disciple appears 274 times in the New Testament—261 times in the Gospels. The word "Christian" only appears in the Bible twice.

The word Christian originated as a derogatory term in the first century. Yet most modern day Christ followers refer to themselves as Christians and not disciples. This is a subtle evidence of the virus. We have moved from the discipleship lifestyle Jesus established, to more of an institutional identification.

Another evidence of the virus is in our view of salvation and conversion. When Jesus commissioned us to "make disciples," He wasn't simply referring to making converts to become cogs in an institutional wheel. We want to make the test for salvation a set of doctrinal positions, rather than embracing the person of Jesus and allowing Him to release the fruit of the Spirit in our lives.

The virus prompts us to trust the practice of repeating a "sinner's prayer" to receive Christ. We also associate "walking the aisle," attending a catechism, or agreeing with a doctrinal/membership statement as evidence that a person is "saved." Those are institutional measurements.

In Scripture, Paul tells us to measure the presence of the "fruit of the Spirit" in a person's life. We have cultivated a generation of church people who think they are Christians when often they are just members of a religious club. Without people demonstrating evidence of the fruit of the Spirit in their lives, we tend to trust ritualized, ecclesiological practices, instead of the Holy Spirit.

The Virus Changed the Meaning

Have you ever tried to converse with a member of a religious cult? It can be maddening. If this has ever happened to you, you know it is possible for each of you to use the same word and be talking about completely different concepts. When someone attaches a different definition to a word it changes its meaning. This subtle shift can be significant.

Church leaders use biblical words and terms with which they're familiar and which have particular definitions. For some reason the meaning of some important words has changed from their meaning as Jesus used them, such as the important words discipleship and multiplication.

When we confuse "discipleship" with doing Bible study, it's easy to believe we are already making disciples in church. When attenders bring their friends to a church service we call that multiplication. How did we get so far from what Jesus was talking about when He said to make disciples?

It's time for a reality check. If you are making disciples, your culture will be growing. However growth does not mean automatically that you are making disciples. If I drive my truck into a muddy bog and it gets stuck, I can press the accelerator and watch the speedometer shoot up to 50 miles per hour. But the reality is I am not going anywhere.

When we are stuck in a non-discipleship culture, revving our engines for all we're worth, we can keep telling ourselves we are making disciples, but the reality is we may still be stuck in version two, using version three language.

Multiplication language has become popular in church circles. Books are written about discipleship; it is the theme of pastors' conferences, and we are using the language of multiplication and discipleship. Neil Cole says, "Unfortunately, when you look more closely you see much of what people call multiplication is really just addition. A church adds a small group, and it is called multiplying. Another worship service is added on Sunday morning, and it is called church multiplication—but it is addition. Adding a venue for worship in your church or a satellite campus is not multiplying a church; it is merely adding." [10]

THE WRONG LABEL

Let's stop using multiplication language inappropriately. We use multiplication language for almost any positive movement in the church. In most cases it is growth by addition at best, often transfer growth from some struggling area church. We seldom see multiplication growth like we read about in the Bible.

We are not reproducing disciples who will reproduce disciples. Such discipleship will produce a movement that will create a significant stir. Most of us have never been a part of a discipleship multiplication movement.

> *"We can't learn something we think we already know."* Alan Hirsch

Why are the words we use to describe the movement important? We will never get to multiplication as long as we keep telling ourselves we already are making disciples who reproduce disciples. We will never become desperate enough to change our behavior before we confront the reality that we have mislabeled what we are currently doing. There is nothing wrong with addition, but it is not multiplication.

---

10 Neil Cole, *Church 3.0*, Jossey-Bass, San Francisco, 2010. p.73

Math is not relative, it is absolute. If you confuse addition with multiplication when you balance your checkbook, your bank will not be amused.

It's Just a Math-Understanding

When I was in school I did not love math. I had no problem with addition or subtraction, but when it came to multiplication and division I struggled – because I refused to learn my multiplication tables. I would rather daydream about sports or any of a hundred different things.

One day, I woke up to the truth that if I didn't learn the multiplication tables, I would never be successful in math. That was the day I was motivated to learn them. The first two math operations—addition and subtraction—are simple, logical, and much easier to learn. When it comes to multiplication, the rapid expansion of the numbers is surprising at first. You need to learn the tables to get a handle on the numbers.

At best our churches simply do addition-level growth by adding one person at a time. You can add the person either by conversion growth or by recruiting him or her from another church.

In the early stage of multiplication, it is impossible to tell if you are multiplying or adding. $2 \times 2 = 4$, and $2 + 2 = 4$. They look identical at first. But you can quickly tell the difference when you keep going. "If you merely add another two to four, the sum is six, and so on. But if you multiply by two you get to eight, then sixteen, and now you know you are multiplying."[11]

Ten calculator key strokes later and you will have 32,768. If you're pressing the addition button, you will just be at 24. The first figure looks like what we read about in the book of Acts. The second sum looks like the average growing US church.

Most of our churches only grow one person at a time. It is obvious we are still doing addition-based growth. If you think about it, addition growth is often produced externally. For example, your church may advertise, do a friend's day push, or do a mission outreach. These situations can create a growth spurt. However, in each situation, the person came from an external source. You are still growing by addition—adding one person at a time.

A distinct set of behaviors is at work when we are still in growth by addition that actually keep us in addition growth. We tend to isolate the new Christ follower and start teaching them Christian information. This phase is what most churches call discipleship. This certainly can be a part of discipleship, but it is not the essence.

Perhaps the new attenders come from a nearby church that is having problems or that even split, scattering its members to other churches. That's not church expansion. Additions you receive from a church in conflict will never produce real growth. It will always hinder your church culture.

---

[11] Ibid, p. 74.

When you make disciples you seed a starfish movement. It starts with investing in personal relationships. How you lead at the beginning will determine if your culture produces multiplication, or simply addition. Yet, investing in discipleship, does not guarantee multiplication.

> *Jesus never used addition to advance the kingdom of God. He build the movement on the principles of multiplication.*

When you concentrate on multiplication, there is a distinct chain of discipling relationships that goes back to the original disciple maker. You will be able to meet new person D, who will be able to say he was discipled by person C, who, in turn, will say she was discipled by person B, who was discipled by person A. The entire process is traceable.

Discipleship Is Not Decontamination

You begin "decontamination" of a new convert when you teach him or her to "act like a Christian." We decontaminate people, instead of discipling them, because we have the virus. Decontamination is what many churches mean when they say they have a discipleship process. Most anthill, tombstone, and house churches decontaminate, rather than disciple a new Christ follower.

When we decontaminate a new convert, we focus on driving them to embrace our set of beliefs or practices. The unintended consequence of this approach is to drive a wedge between the new convert and their potentially disciple-able relationships. This forces them to reject either us or their friends from the culture they just left.

This well-meaning practice removes them from the very process that will grow them as a new Christ follower – reaching back to find disciple-able people from their old community. They don't need to learn to act like a Christian, they need to learn to love Jesus and follow the prompting of the Holy Spirit as He leads them to navigate their past friendships and relationships.

Dangers of Decontamination

Tracy is a beautiful young woman who once was a high-paid Los Angeles prostitute. When she began to follow Jesus, everything in her life changed. She could not stop talking about this new man for whom she had fallen deeply in love. She spoke of Jesus in such personal terms that it caught the attention of other LA call girls she worked with.

Tracy began to make disciples among these women were just as open to Jesus as she was. If she had been decontaminated, she would have become another church person who disappears from "real life." Instead, she went back into the world she had come from and began to share what Jesus was doing for her.

If we decontaminate our disciples and focus on having people like Tracy immediately leave their old friends behind, we actually jerk them out of the real discipleship process Jesus initiated.

Tracy grew as a new follower of Jesus because of the tension she felt as she engaged in spiritual conversations with other call girls. They asked her hard questions for which she had no answers. They were tough on her. She realized she was the personification of what Jesus could do for a person.

If she tried to blend in and be one of them, then they would never ask her about the changes in her life. She realized it takes the power of the Spirit to let others see the changes in her without coming across as disapproving and judgmental. Her biggest motivation to grow as a follower of Jesus came from the questions the other call girls asked. Their questions drove her to look into the Scriptures for answers.

If we had tried to decontaminate Tracy, we would have focused on superficial areas of behavior. We would have counseled her not to associate with other call girls, and would have taught her a set of moral behaviors, such as to have sex only as a married woman. We would have become the voice for the Holy Spirit in her life.

Tracy had been so liberated that she did not want to go back to life on the streets. She was hungry for God's truth that she found in the Bible. Her behaviors did change as the Holy Spirit led her in the process of sanctification. She asked questions about what to do in certain situations. When she asked questions that were inspired by the Holy Spirit, it didn't produce legalism in her. She was searching for the answers. She realized that to have an impact on other women, she had to allow Jesus to keep changing her.

Decontaminating a person's behavior will almost always produce legalism, quench the Spirit and crush the work of making disciples.

Everybody Makes Disciples

I hear pastors say they want to start a discipleship process in their churches. They don't realize they already have one. Oh, it's probably not the one they want, but Jesus assures us discipleship happens all the time. The question is, "What kind of disciples are being made?"

In Matthew 23:15 Jesus exposed the Sadducees' and Pharisees' discipleship process. He said, "Woe to you, teachers of the law and Pharisees, you hypocrites! You travel over land and sea to win a single convert [disciple], and when you have succeeded, you make them twice as much a child of hell as you are."

> *All churches make disciples. The question is. "What kind of disciples are they making?"*

The Sadducees' and Pharisees' disciples assumed they were pleasing to the Father. But Jesus called them children "of hell." Most discipleship systems in our churches are created to increase biblical knowledge and produce behavior correction. Jesus taught His disciples to follow the leading of the Holy Spirit. He spent little time working on moralistic-behavior correction.

Is your church reproducing disciples like we find in the New Testament? Or do your converts simply attend worship on Sunday and small group during the week, listen to Christian radio and come to Christian events? The sad reality is most of these people never become growing disciples who reproduce growing disciples.

THE FACTORY

Think of your church as a discipleship factory. Your raw materials are the people the Holy Spirit drew to you. Many are on a spiritual search for God and for a purpose for their lives.

What is your church factory designed to produce?

The hard question we must face is, "What is coming out of our factories?" Remember, everybody makes disciples and everybody has a factory. What are we producing?

Most of us spend a lot of time and money building and operating the factory. We're very effective at building church services, but then we confuse church services with the work of the church. They are not the same. Disciples don't emerge from our work building church services. When we make disciples, worship becomes a passionate gathering full of life.

What Can a Person Expect
When Entering Our Factories?

When we reproduce viral, contagious Jesus followers, a starfish movement will emerge naturally. Instead, our churches are seduced into meeting consumer demands for quality programs and spiritual services for their children and families. We're trapped into branding ourselves to attract those who are already persuaded and ready to tithe.

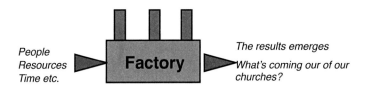

People Resources Time etc. ▶ **Factory** ▶ The results emerges What's coming our of our churches?

The Evangelism Factory

The US church in the late 1980s and early 1990s began to realize a significant part of the Great Commission was missing. We were not being effective at reaching people who were far from Christ. So we shifted focus toward "the seeker." This shift had many benefits, and many people were led to Christ during this season.

The anthill church created an evangelism factory that focused on a new target, but it made a distinction between evangelism and discipleship. These two can't be separated. Evangelism must be an early and integral stage of discipleship. When these two are separated the end product from the factory will be converts, not disciples. Discipleship seldom happens when it becomes one of the factory programs.

Typically, a factory produces one primary product. It will either produce converts or disciples. Converts are often non-reproducing Christians who focus on church attendance and who have associated following Jesus to agreeing with a set of beliefs and sealing it with a prayer.

WE WERE NEVER TO ONLY DO EVANGELISM

Jesus never asked us to do evangelism separately from discipleship. Starfish multiplication creates a discipleship focus that always has evangelism at the front end of discipleship. Jesus always began His relationship with followers by discipling them. He started with individuals who were spiritually open and who had a spiritual hunger. They were all in the category of those not yet convinced.

In most churches, if you ask, "Is discipleship something you do with a Christian or a non-Christian," you'll probably hear that discipleship is something Christians do to grow. Likewise, when we learn to stop separating evangelism and discipleship, we will naturally begin the discipleship process and reach people who are far from Christ and don't know Him. That is what a disciple does.

Our factory must shift from an evangelism factory to a starfish multiplication factory.

Jesus and His followers wouldn't say they were "doing evangelism." Starfish multiplication begins with learning how to initiate and hold spiritual conversations. You can't disciple people until they realize they are far from Christ, and must submit to the leadership of the Holy Spirit. This realization often occurs through spiritual conversations. Romans 10:14 says:

"How can people call for help if they've not been told who to trust? And how can they know who to trust if they haven't heard [the story] of the one who can be trusted? And how can they hear [the story] if no one tells them? And how are they going to tell them [the story], unless someone is sent to do it?"

This passage calls for us to go and share the story that has changed our lives. Instead, we focus on gathering to study the Bible. Often the intention isn't actually to do what it says, only to learn what it says. What if I asked my son to mow the grass, and later that day I find him in the garage with the John Deere manual open and a group of other boys gathered around him?

When I asked him if he understood that I intended for him to mow the grass, he might respond, "Oh, yeah, Dad, I am doing what you asked me to do. I have a group of other yard mowers and we are studying the manual." I would not be pleased with his twisted logic.

How could he think studying the mower manual would be what I asked him to do? This response will not change the height of the grass in my yard. We do the same thing with discipleship. We assume when Jesus asked us to go and make disciples He must have meant He really wanted us to go and study the "manual" with new "manual" readers.

Jesus cut to the heart of this amazing neglect when he asked, "Why do you call me, 'Lord, Lord,' and do not do what I say?" (Luke 6:46–49). James explains when people hear without a plan to act on what they hear, they deceive themselves (James 1:22–23). Reading the Bible is wasted effort if you do not intend to act on it.

> Jesus did not believe that Bible Study alone would make a disciple. If He did, He would have taught all of His disciples to lead Bible studies.

Before Jesus launched His disciple-selection process, He made a strategic decision not to invite any of the "Scripture people" of His time. There was an entire population of people who had dedicated every element of their culture to center on the Scriptures. They built their governmental laws, their economic decisions, and their social customs on what they read in the Scriptures. They were determined to make every part of life conform to the Scriptures.

Jesus not only didn't invite any of them to be His disciples, He confronted them on how off-base they were. He said,

"You study the Scriptures diligently because you think that in them you have eternal life. These are the very Scriptures that testify about me, yet you refuse to come to me to have life."   John 5:39:

It was clear Jesus did not equate discipleship with Scripture study. It was something more.

It seems obvious Jesus was teaching that a person cannot really follow Him without being a disciple who reproduces another disciple (Matthew 28:19–20). This standard should produce great concern to many today who call themselves Christians.

In another passage, Jesus celebrated that His disciples' names were written in the Kingdom of God when they were engaged in discipleship to the third generation. The Christian culture that surrounds us celebrates a person as a Christian when they pray a "sinner's prayer" or learn a catechism.

Remove the Queen

I loved to play video games as a kid. Compared to today, the games of the late 1970s were crude. We had pong and battle tank and a few other low-tech, slow moving games. A kid can only bear so much of hollow kerchunk-kerchunk of the white ping-pong ball hitting the imaginary ping-pong table. Before long we resorted to classic games like chess after we tired of the latest Atari offerings.

I developed a love for chess and, if I may be so bold, I was the best on my street. Well, at least on my side of the street. It was a short street. Really, I never did become a very good chess player.

I made the classic mistake of novice chess players. I usually attempted world domination with the queen. If you don't know much about chess, the queen is the most powerful player on the board. She is not the most important, that is the king. The queen, however, can imitate the movements of most pieces on the board.

The classic mistake novices make is to overuse the queen and underutilize all the other pieces. A chess instructor will remove the queen from the student's arsenal, making him or her learn how to utilize every other piece on the board.

In much the same way, we overuse the weekend service like the poor chess player uses the queen. Pastors are often asked how they teach the Scriptures, or stewardship? How do you cast vision? Where do people come to Christ? How do people serve in your church? Where do people get a sense of community? The list goes on. Most of the time it's the same answer, "The weekend service." Churches utilize the weekend service to accomplish almost everything the church does.

Jesus launched a movement without the queen. He started a starfish movement without a weekend service. This movement was not encumbered with having to produce and execute a weekly event. This allowed the movement to rapidly expand throughout every culture. I don't believe Jesus is opposed to our weekend services, but they do have the ability to distract us from the single commission Jesus gave us.

Church leaders are skilled at gathering people once a week, with much effort to staff, fund, and mobilize Christ followers to attend the service. This service requires program staffing, age-group ministries, stewardship campaigns, and building programs. Most of us intend to make disciples, so the logical question should be: Why is our product so far from what Jesus commissioned us to do?

We produce consumers of church. They shop for the best church product. So we're trapped into continuing to offer the same cafeteria line of options as other churches. This is why few churches ever move from a Sunday morning focus to authentic disciple making that reproduces disciples to the third and fourth generations.

Aiming at the Wrong Target

A story from the 2004 Olympic men's rifle event has become legendary. Matt Emmons was the best chance for the USA to capture gold in this event. He was in the lead to take the gold medal and on his final shot he hit the bull's eye. But it was on the target in the wrong lane!

Four years later, he had a chance to redeem himself in the 2008 Olympics in Beijing. Emmons averaged 10.1 points on his first nine shots in the final round. He only needed to score a 7.0 to take the top spot on the podium. He slowly aimed his rifle deliberately and cautiously. He was obviously nervous, but he was locked in on his target and not the adjacent one. He would be sure not to blow it this time.

He gently squeezed the trigger and launched a shot that completely missed his target. This misfire gave the gold medal to the Chinese athlete. It was hard to believe his over focus and careful deliberation cost him the medal a second time.[12]

This is the mystery of local churches. They are full of good people. Their intentions seem set on the right things. They say they love Jesus. They are focused on teaching the Bible. They pray for people who are far from Christ. Yet they find their efforts are not producing what they had hoped or intended for them to produce. They have mis-aimed.

It's easy to get caught up in the energies and motions of doing church, only to discover we've aimed at the wrong target. Impatience can easily make us miss the process of making disciples who reproduce disciples. Jesus very patiently directed His followers to move toward reproduction. It was not enough for them simply to learn and pass on information. That would have reproduced the rabbinic model of education.

Jesus was focused and He refused to squeeze the trigger at the wrong time and at the wrong target, even as outside pressure built against Him. The Pharisees kept questioning His motives and His intentions, but Jesus was unrelenting. He would not release His disciples until they were ready to reproduce disciples.

---

[12] Steve Rivera, *USA Today*, Gannette News Services, August 17, 2008

The Purpose for Sunday Morning

When our network launches a church, we want to launch it on Day One as a fully functioning discipleship environment on its way to becoming a movement. If the pastor and launch team will take the time to invest in a group of disciples for a season, they will discover they can become a fully functioning discipleship community. They can experience life change and growth. The leaders have to lead well and help the team fight the temptation to become inwardly focused. This is one of the greatest challenges the church-planting leader faces.

The group must stay focused on the mission and on discipling. There will come a time when the group reaches critical mass with a firmly established culture so it can assimilate church attenders. But, the group may choose never to take that step.

At some point, a public launch service can be helpful for the purpose of inviting those who are looking for a church home. If your disciple makers understand that, those who are invited will allow the disciple makers to engage the new attenders in spiritual conversations to identify disciple-able people.

I believe holding a Sunday morning service is primarily to assist your disciple-making leaders in identifying disciple-able people. I believe Jesus held public events for two reasons. First, to hold a *kerygma*, or preaching event, where the truth can be spoken. Disciples often used these events in the New Testament. Jesus, Paul, and the apostles gathered people where the Spirit could move through the public presentation of the gospel.

The second reason to gather on Sunday is to give disciple makers, who have been trained in the process of spiritual conversations, a chance to connect with people whom the Holy Spirit has gathered. I believe this is the primary reason for holding a Sunday morning event.

Most churches can't give a strategic reason for holding Sunday morning services. In many cases, a church plant is really a small group of people who are loyal to the planter. They have come together to help with the set up and take down of equipment and seating for a church service. More often than not the church plant attracts a group of strangers who are disgruntled with their old church situations. This planting team works hard for several hours weekly so an odd collection of strangers can meet together for a service on Sunday morning.

The immediate objective is to gather enough people so the group can take an offering and become financially self-supporting. While the initial objective may to be reach people who are far from God, it doesn't take long to realize the people they intended to reach haven't come to the Sunday morning services. Before long, they realize the only way to reach those who are far from God is to build relationships with them one person at a time.

The best approach is to shift the new group's limited resources toward focusing on making disciples, instead of launching a church service. This way when they do hold a service they are launching a church instead of launching a Sunday service full of strangers.

PART TWO

Culture That Launches

A Starfish Movement

STARFISH

CHAPTER 5

LAUNCHING A STARFISH NETWORK

Most denominations tend to focus on planting churches rather than launching movements. Church-planting pastors say they have a vision to start many churches from that first plant.

What they mean is that when the new church grows to where they have too many people for their facility, have enough money, and extra time and staff resources, then they will launch the next church. That seldom happens. I call that approach, "We will start a church when...." They are waiting on a predetermined set of circumstances to drive reproduction. God has designed us to reproduce from our DNA. This is the core of starting a starfish movement. It must come from DNA.

Josh was a church planter who embraced the classic church-planter vision of launching a church that would birth others. He began with the classic anthill church-plant approach. After a year, not only had he not planted another church, but he was ready to quit the one he had started. I suggested that Josh go back through the training he had attended only out of obligation and try to figure out what went wrong. This time he got it. He was desperate enough to make the sacrifices to launch a real starfish movement and it was amazing to see the transformation.

He was a different leader. The pressure for him to perform was off. He was able to empower others to release a multiplication culture. When he was in the anthill mode, I asked him how many leaders he had that he could disciple. He honestly said there were none. Within one year of operating in a starfish mode, he launched three campuses and trained six more leaders who would soon be ready to launch campuses with disciples and more multiplication. This is what happens when you shift focus from the anthill to the starfish paradigm.

When Josh made the shift, he made everything revolve around the singular focus of making disciples. He eliminated all elements that competed with reproduction and moved to full mission alignment. Churches that make this shift must be fiercely intentional about reproduction. Churches that successfully move to full alignment have very little internal conflict.

Getting to that place will not be smooth. Don't be surprised if some people leave when your church shifts from anthill to starfish approach. Once you make this shift, though, things will smooth out.

Conflict usually focuses on the de-emphasis of the Sunday morning service, which most Christians make what I call an unnecessary priority. This service is not a bad thing from a biblical viewpoint, but it is not as valued in the Scriptures as we have inflated it to be. Do you think church is about what occurs in the Sunday morning service?

In our network, we don't invest our first energy into establishing a Sunday service. We put our first energy toward disciple making. It is amazing how rich worship events can be when vibrant disciples gather. When we focus on discipleship, it takes little effort to start a worship service. A disciple living a transformed life will naturally desire to gather for times of worship and connection. He will gladly serve and contribute when he has been changed by the Spirit of God.

One Life Church is a millennial church plant in Knoxville, Tenn. led by Rodney Arnold and Tyler Goode. They have launched one of the best attractional church plants I've ever seen. Tyler is the man behind the scenes who makes all the technical magic happen. He is focused on producing the perfect combination of sound, lighting and video. Rodney leads well as the pastor.

Rodney had a great start, but the new plant plateaued after a year during the mid-2000s. Rodney is an amazingly gifted leader who had prepared for the launch better than any pastor I have ever worked with. Despite all his preparation, the church was stuck.

Rodney decided to engage himself fully to shift the culture from anthill to starfish, embracing everything necessary to make it happen.

God began to change Rodney and the things Rodney cares about changed. Rodney fiercely aligned the church around discipleship multiplication. This change required Tyler to make some serious changes, or be left behind. I have never seen a technically oriented leader make the radical changes Tyler made. He embraced the new culture and began to make disciples.

You might suppose the shift away from production and performance would drop the quality of the worship event. Tyler shifted from sole focused on producing an attractional church service to investing time and energy making disciples. The new disciples came from the artist community of musicians and techies. The quality of the worship went up because Tyler invested in cultivating a discipleship culture among those people groups.

> *"A rising tide lifts all boats."* John F Kennedy

Rodney was the reason for this change in Tyler. He is a gifted directional leader, but he decided to turn his attention Tyler and invest in him as his first disciple. Rodney's leadership decision to put discipleship first changed everything in the church.

John F. Kennedy said, "A rising tide lifts all boats." One Life made discipleship multiplication its primary focus, yet the worship experience is amazing because the disciples enjoy serving together as they invest in the lives of other talented musicians and leaders.

CHAPTER 6

THE BRIQUETTES MUST HEAT UP.

The first warm day after we married, my wife decided it was time for me to apply my man skills. She decided I needed to cook outdoors. Of course, she did all the hard work: she went out and bought the charcoal and lighter fluid. She bought the hamburger meat and put it all together for me.

I didn't tell her I had never grilled before because I didn't want her to think she married a guy with no man card. So I did what any guy without a clue does: I faked it. Acting like I knew what I was doing I spread all the briquettes out on the grill surface, and soaked them with lighter fluid. Expecting quick results, I put a match to the fuel but succeeded only in burning off the lighter fluid. I repeated the process until the bottle of fluid was empty.

The only problem was the briquettes were still black and cool. I knew the charcoal needed to turn white hot to cook the meat. We eventually ate the burgers that night, despite their strong chemical taste. The good news is we did not die from eating chemically treated meat that was nearly raw.

I finally learned that you start a fire in a barbecue grill by putting the briquettes in a pile so the heat from one ignites another. Without this step, the briquettes will never burn white hot. A briquette won't become a hot coal without contact with other briquettes.

The Holy Spirit Heats Up A Culture of Life Change

Look at the barbecue process to discern some critical elements of launching a discipleship culture. Jesus took a small group who were open to the working of God's Spirit and piled them together so they could heat each other up. He poured the Holy Spirit on them and before long they began to glow. He spread them out and they continued to heat things up all over the world. That is the New Testament story in a nutshell.

Becoming White Hot

You can launch a starfish movement in your community. As with the briquettes, the key is to first find Christ followers who have a potential to transmit heat. That is what Jesus did.

Start with those who show evidence that the Holy Spirit is at work in their lives. In the first church they identified leaders who were, "known to be full of the Spirit and wisdom" Acts 6:3. The criteria in the first *ecclesia* was the presence of the Holy Spirit in the life of the potential disciple maker.

> *Jesus set the world on fire with a small group of 12 briquettes.*

The second quality was wisdom. In the Scriptures, wisdom is a result of the indwelling of the Spirit that leads and directs life decisions. It doesn't take long to begin to display Spirit-led wisdom. There are many examples of changes that occur when the Spirit works in a person's life. It may show up in a how a person feels the need to get out of debt. The Spirit may prompt a person to seek forgiveness, or handle conflict differently or to live as a kinder, gentler, wiser person. All of these changes come from the presence of the Spirit in a person's life.

When you launch this kind of strategic gathering it can become the genesis of a discipleship movement. Something amazing happens when you put Christ followers together whose lives have been changed by the Holy Spirit. They begin to inspire and challenge each other.

In the churches we have planted we call this process Xcellerate. It is the primary vehicle we use to reproduce disciples.

What is Xcellerate?

Xcellerate is our discipleship process. The "X" in our name relates to my endless hours in algebra class. The missing element of an algebraic equation is represented by the letter X. The missing piece in our churches is the discipleship process that Jesus gave us.

The middle portion of the name is "cell." Jesus used the principle of the briquettes to heat up His group of disciple-able leaders. Likewise, we intentionally put together the potential briquettes that the Spirit of God leads us to. When they are together, they heat each other up and create an atmosphere you cannot craft any other way.

The last portion of the name "erate" means to increase the speed of something, or to multiply the process. In the Gospels we see Jesus making disciples and confronting the spiritual deficiency in the Jewish religious system of His time. Jesus was solving the "X" problem. He launched a discipleship multiplication culture as the core of everything He did. He assembled potential disciples in a "cell" environment. Then He invested His best energies developing this group. He created discipleship tension so that they would grow and develop in the culture He had produced. This was His "eration" process. He was intensifying the process for them.

We launch our churches with the discipleship process first, before we get distracted by myriad other details that accompany leading a church. We carefully select disciple-able individuals who we believe are open to the leading of the Holy Spirit. We begin to invest time and energy training this group in the ways of Kingdom-oriented starfish discipleship. It can take up to two years just to detox them from the culture they have come from.

When an Xcellerate leader finishes three years of training, he or she will be able to see life through a biblical lens. He or she will have established discipling relationships that are multiplying. In many cases they may be leading an *ecclesia* of reproducing disciples.

> *"The greatest issue facing the world today, is whether those who identify as "Christians" will actually reproduce Jesus with their life..."* Dallas Willard

If they are directional leaders, they will be in a development-training process to launch a multiplication culture. As a result, the leaders will be more confident and bold in their walks with Christ. They will be able to share in the Kingdom advance that is so essential for the Church to be effective in the world.

The Xcellerate approach doesn't focus on a curriculum or a memorized speech to initiate spiritual conversations. Our Xcellerators realize that almost any conversation can be a spiritual conversation. We will discuss later how to cultivate and develop spiritual conversations. The goal of spiritual conversations is not to persuade a stranger to pray a prayer or make a spiritual commitment. Spiritual conversations are designed to identify disciple-able people who will become committed Christ followers.

Jesus Formed an Xcellerate Group

I believe Jesus launched the first Xcellerate group with the smallest unit for discipleship. He established a relationship with John. Jesus identified John as "low-hanging fruit" since John already was connected to the Essenes, a group spiritually sensitive to the promptings of God. They studied Scripture in an area outside of Jerusalem near the fortress of Masada in the Qumran caves. This group produced the writings that, once discovered, became known as the "Dead Sea scrolls."

Jesus did an interesting thing in John's discipleship process. He empowered John by allowing John to baptize Him, thus legitimizing John and including him as a cornerstone in the starfish movement.

Jesus submitted Himself to the ways of the Essene culture that John was leading. I believe He did this to connect and relate to other leaders. After John baptized Jesus, we see a shift in his approach. John began naturally to have spiritual conversations with others related to his new relationship with Jesus. He said in John 1:26, "Among you [Jesus] stands one you do not know...the straps of whose sandals I am not worthy to untie."

Jesus continued to cultivate the connections he made through John. When it came time to select potential disciples He began with friends from John's culture. In John 1:35 it says:

"The next day John was there again with two of his disciples. When he saw Jesus passing by, he said, 'Look, the Lamb of God!' When the two disciples heard him say this, they followed Jesus. Turning around, Jesus saw them following and asked, 'What do you want?' They said, 'Rabbi, where are you staying?' 'Come,' he replied, 'and you will see.'"

Jesus met one discipleship candidate and watched the connection spread to the next. John says a couple of verses later in John 1:40, "Andrew, Simon Peter's brother, was one of the two who heard what John had said and who had followed Jesus. The first thing Andrew did was to find his brother Simon and tell him."

The spiritual conversations spread through the community of followers that John gathered. Jesus, Andrew and Simon spent time together. The second group formed the next day. Jesus was moving His operation north to the Galilee region. (John 1:43).

Nathaniel was not as easily convinced as the others were. He responded, "Nazareth! Can anything good come from there?" Nathaniel let what he knew about the locals get in the way. He knew Nazareth was a small commuter town for the larger regional city of Sepphoris. Carpenters who lived there commuted into the city to work on Roman construction projects. They were building the huge new amphitheater at that time.

Jesus knew when He saw Nathanael that he was struggling to believe Jesus was the Messiah. Jesus began by saying, "'Here, truly is an Israelite in whom there is no deceit.' 'How do you know me?' Nathanael asked. Jesus answered, 'I saw you while you were still under the fig tree before Philip called you,'" (John 1:47–49).

When I read this the first hundred times, I didn't get what just happened. The word Jesus used when He said, "I saw you," is the phrase that means to look into, to know deeply, to have an inner knowledge of. Jesus just told him: I know that you were praying a few minutes ago because I really do know you.

In another setting, when Jesus had moved up to the seashore, He launched His third Xcellerate group. He saw James and John and invited them. (Matthew 4:21).

> "All who are called to salvation are
> called to multiply disciples, no exceptions,
> no excuses!"   Bill Hull

In these situations Jesus is forming relationships in small groups of three. Jesus spoke about the power of doing discipleship in small groups in Matthew 18:20: "Where two or three gather in my name, there am I with them." There is something powerful about getting together in groups of three.

A typical modern pattern for discipleship is one on one. Jesus never did any of His discipleship strategy one-on-one. He always led groups of two or more. He spent the majority of His time in groups of six to twelve. Group size makes a difference. While it seems a one-on-one format would be easier to lead than a group of three to five it's actually easier to lead a larger group because group members provide energy and momentum.

One on one is the most difficult to lead because the leader feels all the pressure to be the teacher. The disciple quickly adopts the role of student. It takes a skilled leader to lead a one-on-one discipleship setting a skill most will not develop. Research suggests most one-on-one discipleship relationships last only a few sessions. As a result, new Christ followers are not getting a very solid start in building a biblical worldview.

Every disciple has the ability to make a disciple almost immediately—if they are grown in a discipleship community that is based on a group size of three to five. Naturally, as this process unfolds, the groups will expand to as many as six. When a group gets to six, it's time to identify a new leader and start a new group.

"We can do more with 12 disciples than with 12,000 religious consumers." Alan Hirsch

This is a simpler process than you imagine. The new group forms around the person who is most instrumental to the development of the new batch of disciples. The Xcellerate groups stay connected and meet in small clusters for convenience and efficiency. It's much easier to find a meeting time when you only have to negotiate three or four schedules.

When Xcellerate groups take shape around naturally formed people groups, they will reproduce more effortlessly. This is how Jesus bonded with the disciples of John. These groups naturally reproduced as new leaders were cultivated and as new bonded relationships emerged. We will discuss this more in the "How to Reach the *Oikos*" section.

Most of Us Are Not Ready For Multiplication

Most churches are not ready for rapid-addition growth. The truth is we are not even ready for slow, gradual addition growth. Consider what would be required if you had two hundred people added to your church this week. You would be doing cartwheels at first, but what would you have to do to care for that many more children and adults?

What would a church do if it really multiplied and had 5,000 people come to Christ this month? What if next month it reached 10,000? How long would it take before your model for doing church would no longer work? What facility would you rent to accommodate those numbers?

> *"Does the gospel I preach have a natural tendency to cause people to become sold out to follow Jesus?"* Dallas Willard

Of course, we think it would be great to multiply, but what would you do to care for all those people who would come looking to you for answers? Under the Version 2 model it would require an extensive building campaign, three hundred acres, and hundreds of millions of dollars.

Even if your church experienced the amazing growth that I just mentioned, it still would not make a dent in the population of most of our towns and cities. Our expectations are so small in comparison to what it would take to really reach our communities.

We've all heard people say their church is multiplying like crazy. You know if you've read this far that they're likely taking about a gradual addition. Even in this mode, it would not be long before that church encounters the classic growth hurdles that modest addition can bring. If we did begin to multiply, most of us would try to solve the new problems with Version 2 style answers, a solution that is costly, time consuming and very slow.

The New Testament church followed the leading of the Holy Spirit and multiplied rapidly. That multiplication culture empowered many new disciple makers. Jesus' plan to care for and develop these new disciples was decentralized and didn't depend on hierarchal decision-making. They kept it simple. The process didn't depend on an institution or finances to solve its issues. These are all starfish qualities.

MULTIPLICATION IS FRAGILE

I have experienced real discipleship multiplication twice: once at Daybreak, the church we planted in Carlsbad, Calif., and again at Beach Church in Myrtle Beach, SC. Both cases required several years to create a culture where multiplication could emerge. These seasons were exciting and stressful at the same time. It was exhilarating to see lives change and growth occur.

However, multiplication momentum is fragile. In both cases we were amazed at the work of the Holy Spirit. But I unwittingly fell back into leadership behaviors that prevented the movement from continuing to expand. I have spent most of my life in Version 2 churches. So what happened?

After I established the essential elements to launch a starfish movement the discipleship culture began to multiply and disciples naturally reproduced disciples. Empowered leaders began to reproduce new leaders. But, as the church multiplied I tried to solve growth issues with the wrong set of solutions.

My mentors encouraged me to hire consultants to help us raise money to build, but this distracted us from the very thing that was producing our growth. In both churches we made a wrong U-turn and reverted to anthill solutions to starfish tensions.

I led the churches to do what most churches do: add support staff, hire ministry professionals, and build buildings to accommodate the growth. With each step, our momentum began to shift. We continued to grow, but the momentum of multiplication began to subside as I turned my attention to leading the staff and constructing buildings. My leadership decisions led us back to growth by addition even though we had tasted multiplication growth and found it sweet. We eventually became content with more manageable transfer growth, settling for addition over multiplication.

I became content to reach one person at a time. I enjoyed the slower, steady growth because it was easier on me, my family and the staff. I realize now that I had sabotaged what God was doing in favor of something I could handle.

The most obvious shift was the stories people were sharing. The people we were attracting were different. Typically, they were no longer new Christ followers with a radical life transformation, but were Christians from other churches who had heard about our exciting life-change stories.

They came to us talking about problems at their old churches, and how we were a better option for their families. Their stories were more about how much of a better church experience we were offering than other churches.

> "The Father has not promised to bless our good motives, dreams and innovations. He promised to bless His plan; that plan is that disciples make other disciples - everything else is a sideshow." *Bill Hull*

Starfish movements naturally grow. If they are allowed to grow without excessive control and top-down organization, they will remain vibrant and strong. However, if the leader applies Version 2 solutions to problems, the very elements that created the multiplication environment will be deflated and the movement quickly flattened. I was surprised at how fast a multiplying church can revert to anthill ways.

We had become the cool church. Our growth gave us access to better musicians and our new included the best children's ministry space possible. We acquired land where the population was growing, so we were convenient to new families. We were winning a competition for bodies and budget that I didn't even know we were waging. I had become distracted, and as a result, the church was distracted.

There is an unstated competition among local churches, which discover that incremental improvements can attract people from other churches. I believe we are approaching the end of this church competition. The Millennial generation is not shopping for a better church experience. They want something more than the superficial accoutrements put in place by churches battling for the suburban family with 2.3 children who arrive in an SUV. Baby Boomers and Gen Xers are the ones still swayed by church competition. Christians in these age groups have flocked to the local church that is growing and alive.

This kind of church competition is a horrible detriment to actual multiplication growth. An influx of new attenders who bring their previous church culture with them can take a multiplying church off mission. This kind of competition for families will likely continue for a few years, but a number of factors will shift the discussion soon. Among them: Millennials' lack of interest in the institutional church, increasing secularism, and an increasingly hostile environment toward the institutional church, will require a different approach. This presents a great opportunity for us to focus more clearly on what Jesus called us to do in the first place—make disciples our first focus.

Multiplication versus Addition Growth

Growth presents challenges, rather by multiplication or addition.

Multiplication growth occurs among people who are far from Christ. They usually have no church background, come with messy lives and don't always clean up quickly. Often, they have a crazy past that includes addictions and debt.

Addition growth usually occurs from Christians who are looking for a better church experience. They often appear less messy at first, but if they are going to be trained to reproduce disciples, they will require a long season of church-culture detox. This group often brings a legalistic set of values that can be one of the most difficult mindsets to change.

If the starfish movement is to thrive, the leader must fight the temptation to be a leadership bottleneck, insisting that all decisions pass through him or her. The shift to decentralize leadership is not easy for leaders steeped in the anthill school of leadership. If the culture is to multiply in every part of its being, leaders must empower other leaders who can expand and launch movements.

Where the Leader Looks
Is Where the Culture Goes

This principle applies to most adventure sports. When you snowboard, skateboard, or whitewater kayak, you will go where you're looking. This is especially true when you are paddling through a whitewater rapid—the direction you turn your head is the direction the kayak immediately turns. Likewise, a church leader's focus sets the direction for his or her church.

As I mentioned earlier, I turned my attention away from multiplication in two different settings where we had launched a starfish multiplication movement. We grew rapidly and then came cultural Christians who brought the virus with them. I unintentionally allowed the addition virus to infect the multiplication culture and I ended up spending my best energies managing the growth instead of releasing the growth.

The first time we planted 10 churches, but they didn't come out of the multiplication culture. They were classic Version 2 church plants and satellites.

When we started growing rapidly, I sought council from the leaders of large, growing churches. They recommended I control the growth and I took their advice. I had no other models since I had never seen a starfish movement. At the time, the Version 3 church in Asia was just emerging. Even today, there are very few examples of how to translate the starfish model into a context that works. By following the advice of leaders of US mega churches I crushed what God had begun in me by becoming the leadership bottleneck in the new culture. The council of Jesus in Matthew 6:24 is: "No one can serve two masters...he will hate the one and love the other."

Jesus warned that a leader cannot successfully move in two directions at the same time. One master will tug harder. Trying to move in two directions at once only creates conflict. Version 3 leadership is not simply Version 2 executed better. The versions are completely different and incompatible. Even the Son of God didn't try to lead a multiplication movement out of the prevalent Jewish culture. He said, "Do not think that I have come to abolish the Law or the Prophets; I have not come to abolish them but to fulfill them" (Matthew 5:17). Jesus was not embracing the chaotic Jewish culture; He was setting it straight.

How Do I Start A Starfish Movement?

Whether you are a church planter with a hand full of people on your core team, or you lead an established church, you basically start the same way. The five principles for launching a starfish multiplication culture are gleaned from the first starfish movement. If these five principles are not present, a multiplication culture likely will not emerge. Paul and the apostles used them to launch churches throughout the Roman empire. They are:

1. The art of spiritual conversations
2. Identify a person of peace
3. Teach persons of peace to reach the *oikos*
4. Build a Jesus worldview
5. Reproduce the culture

These core principles center on creating behaviors that reproduce disciples. Nothing happens without identifying a disciple-able person. When you embrace Jesus' core principles, follow the leading of the Holy Spirit, and learn from the new disciple, you will discover the necessary skills to launch a starfish culture.

Embracing a multiplying, discipleship culture is a process. If you lead a group entrenched in a culture with established traditions be patient. Don't suddenly announce that, "Things are going to change around here," and take them off in a new direction.

Don't approach discipleship as a program. You will need to continue to care for the group you have inherited while laying the foundation and identifying disciple-able candidates. If you currently are in ministry you should view care for your current members as your tent-making job. This work is your income while you launch a discipleship culture.

Occupying a stale ministry position is like a church planter working bi-vocationally to provide income while he builds a new church plant. You likely have some in the church who are ready to be part of a new multiplication culture. Don't become discouraged by the ones who are entrenched in church culture. Identify the disciple-able ones, and help them detox from the virus elements they previously embraced.

Try to refocus what your church already is doing. Some elements of routine can be repurposed. In most cases the problem is not their behaviors. The problem is the intense church work effort that keeps them so busy they have no time or energy to make an impact. Can you repurpose an outreach event to be a contact event? Even the Sunday morning service can be refocused eventually to advance a disciple-making culture. There is no inherent value in just producing a Sunday morning service if it doesn't advance the work of the Kingdom.

Churches seem convinced that Jesus called us to put on events. Events will have no impact if a disciple making culture is not in place to connect with potential new disciples.

Remember, a multiplication culture doesn't emerge from preaching sermons and launching programs. Jesus used public speaking to build a foundation of credibility for the disciples who would soon go through the towns and villages identifying disciple-able people.

> *"Jesus poured His life into a few disciples and taught them to reproduce other disciples. Seventeen times we find Jesus with the masses, but forty-six times we see Him with His disciples."* Dann Spader

As we were planting our first church in San Diego, Calif., our sponsor church recommended we do an outreach event at the local mall using its choir to sing carols at Christmastime. The church's excellent choir had been featured on the local news and the church viewed these outreach events as a success. We accepted their offer to help.

As the choir sang, shoppers paused briefly, then walked around us because we were in their way. The reality is our 50-member choir was slowing them down from their Christmas shopping.

We handed out invitations to our Sunday services. That was it; that's all we did. Our "outreach event" was just a bunch of religious people standing and singing songs live that were already playing over the sound system. We spoke to no one. No relationships were initiated. Everyone simply ignored us. It was the most important message people would hear all day, yet we had presented it in the most irrelevant manner imaginable.

Churches still take this approach, though, because they haven't shaken the virus. The Christian thought process is very different from the secular way of thinking. We don't see how naïve and simple we can come across. We've lived so long in our bubble that we don't realize our normal behavior is odd, quaint or irrelevant to the secular culture.

Try to be patient with church folks you have inherited. They need time to detox and begin to see the starfish culture take hold. Since church attendance has been the barometer of how Christianity is doing for so long it will take time to make this shift. Ultimately, a starfish culture results in life transformation. It is not enough to fill our churches; we must transform our world. If the church is effective, we should see a change in society and culture.

The following chapters present the five necessary principles for launching a starfish culture in your setting.

Starfish

CHAPTER 7

THE ART OF SPIRITUAL CONVERSATIONS

PRINCIPLE ONE

When Canadian race car driver George Robson was asked how he won the Indy 500, he said it was simple.

"All I had to do was keep turning left," he said.[13]

The Starfish movement principles of disciple making are simple; all we have to do is learn how to have effective spiritual conversations and the process will emerge. Spiritual conversations are the

---

[13] George Robson, retrieved from www.thinkexist.com/ quotes

tool by which we identify disciple-able people. When the new disciple engages in spiritual conversations they will face questions for which they have no answers. You will lead them to find answers in the Scriptures and they will develop a hunger for those answers and their source.

It begins with simply having a spiritual conversation about Jesus. This is the foundation block for making a disciple. If the process doesn't start with spiritual conversations it won't start at all. By Jesus and following Him our focus we avoid all the pitfalls associated with dogma, doctrines and denominations.

Spiritual Conversations Reveal Disciple-able People

Spiritual conversations are the most valuable tool for making disciples. They were the primary tool of the early church, which had no Bible, little training and less organization. They held no events for the curious. Jesus' style was engaging daily in spiritual conversations. He launched His movement by teaching His disciples the art of listening to the Holy Spirit as they engaged in such conversations.

One day as I was reading again about the original starfish movement in the book of Acts, I noticed something I had never seen before. When this group of ordinary, working class followers boldly shared their story and engaged in spiritual conversations, the Holy Spirit seemed to show up and create life change. Then I noticed how many times it said they "shared boldly" what God had done. I noticed in Acts 2:42 that new followers were engaging in spiritual conversations.

It says, "They devoted themselves to share the <u>apostles' teaching</u>." This would have been in the form of a spiritual conversation about what the apostles had shared with them. Because they had no Bibles or written instructions, virtually everything they knew about the Kingdom of God came from spiritual conversations.

> *The movement that Jesus birthed, primarily moved forward based on the spiritual conversations His followers had with those who were far from Christ.*

You may say that now we read the Bible instead of having spiritual conversations. In both cases the information is transferred, but the two methods are very different. Relationships develop through conversation, which establishes the foundation for discipling. Their only tool for creating life change was spiritual conversations.

I began to notice how frequently early Christ followers engaged in spiritual conversations. In most cases they were simply talking about Jesus and sharing their story. Eventually I noticed an odd pattern. Almost every time a spiritual conversation occurred in the book of Acts it was in a verse 42. This was a strange coincidence. I call this the principle of the "forty-twos."

I underlined the conversation words in the passages where the principle of the "forty two's" occurs. Acts 5:42 says, "Day after day...they never stopped <u>speaking about</u> and <u>sharing</u> the amazing news about Jesus." They were armed with nothing more than their personal account of how Jesus had changed their lives.

Acts 9:42 says, "They <u>spoke</u> of what God had done all over Joppa, and many people believed in the Lord."

New followers emphatically <u>proclaimed</u> in Acts 10:42, "The Father compelled us to <u>speak</u> about these things to the people and to share our story, that Jesus is the one whom God appointed as judge of the living and the dead."

Even as they engaged the religious elite they found favor. "As they were leaving the synagogue, the leaders invited them to <u>speak</u> further about the things God was up to the next time they gathered" (Acts 13:42).

> *Spiritual conversations must center on the story of how Jesus has impacted the life of the Christ follower.*

These verses show us how a group of Christ followers devoted themselves to speak and share bravely about the one who had changed them. They shared their personal story and they examined the way Jesus refocused some common fishermen to live a Kingdom-centered life.

Spiritual conversations must center on the story of Jesus, as told through your experience with Him.

This group didn't have influence or credentials. They didn't start with anything that would give them credibility or recognition. All they had was their life change stories and the spiritual conversations that came as the Holy Spirit led them.

THE POWER OF A STORY

People's stories fascinate us. Most successful movies and TV shows are simply about a person's story. Reality shows are nothing more than the unfolding of a supposedly unscripted story in real time.

People listen to things that reach them emotionally and personally. When we share our story from our heart, people pay attention. When we try to force an intellectual truth on someone, they recoil. Learning to tell your story will be an essential part of creating a starfish culture. It will also become the vehicle God will use to grow you as a disciple.

> "Knowing how to tell a compelling story is always at the center of how a culture and tribe are built."   *Steve Jobs*

We may never be the person people gather around at a party. We may not be asked to share our story with the media. But as a Christ follower, you have a powerful story to share. Too many

Christ followers have a sense of inadequacy that makes them shrink away from sharing their stories.

The power of your story is that God has engaged Himself in your life! Focus on His work in you. He is giving you an ongoing story for today, tomorrow and the next day. The art of testimony is that God will fuse what you read in the Scriptures with an example from your current life. The key is to learn to fit those two things together. Your story becomes powerful at the intersection of your life and Scripture.

The first step is to look prayerfully for a person who can be discipled. Use the process of spiritual conversation to find this person. Talk about Jesus and about your story with others. Look for people who are searching and spiritually open. You will soon discover the Holy Spirit provides opportunities for you to share a brief story that can lead to further conversation.

The key word here is *brief*. Keep in mind that people are not interested in every detail of your life, or every intricacy of your story. This is a chance to tell a non-weird God story that relates to the conversation topic.

Christians are notorious for telling weird God stories. We do so because we've been trained to do so. If you spend any time around a group of Christians it's not long before someone shares a genuinely powerful story of how God moved in a situation. Among like-minded believers, a "weird" God story is not so weird. It can provide encouragement and insight to those who understand.

But, telling the same story among people not inclined to sift through the odd elements of God's power, and you have a weird God story that leaves them cold. Let's face it; most Christians are bad at sorting out the weird elements of their stories. It's painful enough for us to listen to well-meaning Christ followers stumble through tedious retellings of events that include way too many unnecessary details. Imagine how it is to those far from God to stroll down spiritual memory lane that seems more like a nightmare on Elm Street.

Jesus was the best at telling stories that had no weird God element to them. In Luke 15 He tells a story that shows the love of God by using the example of a father who allows his adult son the scary freedom to choose his own path because he loves him. The story reveals the horrible decisions the son made.

Jesus reminds us that son's bad decisions did not diminish the father's his love. The story was brief, but powerful. Jesus created spiritual conversations with the story. This is a method He used to jumpstart spiritual conversations.

Advertisers will tell you the single most persuasive ad is always the personal testimony. When a person stands before the camera and says, "I was fluffy and now look at me, I lost 55 pounds," it gets our attention. Each of us is trying to process how life works. We fear bad things happening to us. A personal story has a powerful life change element. It gets our attention.

See it in John 9 when a man who had lived with a debilitating handicap is healed. He tells his story in 12 words. He knew only what he had experienced. He hadn't learned about Jesus yet, but he said, "One thing I do know. I was blind but now I see" (John 9: 25). It was brief and personal.

Each of us has the story of our experience with Christ. His work in your life is the most influential part of your spiritual conversation. It is significant in your growth and growing confidence to sort through your story and uncover where and when God began His work in you. This will be the first major step in becoming a reproducing disciple – identifying your story and sharing it.

Remember, we share our stories to cultivate a spiritual conversation. We are not trying to do anything other than find disciple-able people. This is a different approach from classic evangelism. Historically, Christians have been focused primarily on starting a conversation that was focused on leading a person to pray the "sinner's prayer." We want to have spiritual conversations to discover who is disciple-able, and then build a relationship with them—not to "close the deal."

*"The world is not made of atoms.
It is made of stories." - Muriel Ruykeser*

Learn to Tell Your Story/Testimony

It was a crisp fall day when I showed up at the gym to pursue my goal of playing basketball for Georgetown College. But something happened that day to forever change my life. I went up for a defensive rebound and caught an elbow to the face that broke my cheekbone and nose. I needed surgery to reconstruct that part of my face, but it was what happened next that changed everything for me.

The anesthesiologist used cocaine to sedate me for the surgery. My body reacted to the drug and I went into cardiac arrest. Doctors used a defibrillator three times to get my heart beating again. During the time I was unconscious, I had a taste of eternity and that experience had a dramatic impact on me. I had come face to face with my mortality.

I became hungry to know more about eternity. I began to read the Gospel accounts of Jesus. They were new and fresh to me since I had never seen them before. This Jesus I was discovering was amazing. He was the very thing I was thirsting for. As I read I embraced the Holy Spirit. This was not an experience with religion; this was personal. I learned in the Scriptures about eternity, but it was more than that. Jesus set my life in a new direction.

The presence of the Holy Spirit was the most significant part of my story. I had no prior knowledge of the Holy Sprit before that point. My experience was personal, and it didn't fit easily into any easy category. I simply had met Jesus and now everything was different. It had nothing to do with religion or church. In fact, Jesus almost seemed separate from either of those two realms. That is how I came to trust Jesus, and how He reached out to me.

Two Types of Testimonies

Every Christ follower has two types of stories or testimonies. There is the life change story, which is the original *Christ-encounter story*. The encounter usually has elements of spiritual submission and repentance.

The second type of testimony is the ongoing *story based around a God truth*. When most Christ followers hear the term *testimony* they usually think of the former type of story. We need to expand the definition to include more than the details around conversion. If we learn how to adapt your ongoing story it can be a powerful tool to open spiritual conversations.

Listen to the Holy Spirit. Learn to find appropriate opportunities to apply your story and use it in the right way. Finding a gracious way to connect your story to the person you are talking to requires a little skill and the leading of the Holy Spirit.

The Christ Encounter Story

I had been snowboarding all day when I decided to take one last run before heading home. My plan was to avoid people, scream down one last run, and bust it home. I had already said goodbye to my group and I was on my own, no schedule other than returning home.

I was getting onto the high-speed quad to go up the mountain, when at the last second a couple glided into the open spots and joined me. They both had warm smiles and seemed friendly enough. We exchanged nods and put the lap bar down. I clicked on my tunes and zoned out.

About two minutes into the ride, the lift jerked hard and suddenly stopped. We all acknowledged that what just happened didn't feel right. We started talking about a potential long delay and before long we were involved in a full-blown conversation. I assumed they were from India and were probably Hindu. I asked them where their families were from. They confirmed my assumptions and I told them they seemed to be from the southern part of the country.

They lit up and asked me how I had guessed correctly. I told them I had spent some time in southern India and they had some of the characteristics of the region. It turned out I had spent time in their very neighborhood. This opened up an entire new level of conversation. They seemed excited to talk with someone who knew about their home.

They told me I seemed to love their country and wondered why I had such an interest in their home. I literally felt the tug of the Holy Spirit. Here's an opening: He was nudging me to carefully follow Him into this conversation. I hadn't planned a spiritual conversation, but the Holy Spirit had other plans. It was like the Spirit was saying, "I love these people and I want them to see me through you. You need to be careful here."

In the very short time I had been with this couple, my heart had expanded toward them. I could tell I had favor with them as well.

I wondered how life really was for them and whether or not they were fulfilled. I was curious about where they were spiritually. I had no idea where this conversation was headed, but I quietly hoped I'd be able to be a part of their spiritual journey.

"When I went to India I didn't know what to expect," I said. "I was surprised at how God had given me a love for the people there in a very short time." They asked me, "Why do you think that is?" This was my chance, I had to be careful not to try to trounce on a small spark of interest.

"There was a time when I didn't have much interest in anyone but myself," I said. "I had little tolerance for people who were different from me. I had a spiritual encounter with Jesus that changed my life."

They both just sat there for a moment. I wasn't sure what was happening. Had I over shared? Had I rushed in too soon? Was I listening well enough to the leading of the Spirit? Their silence was killing me. It was probably only four seconds, but it felt like an hour.

Then one of them said, "Yeah, I have heard people talk like that about this Jesus guy. We worship Jesus as an idol, but I don't know much about Him, really." I asked him to tell me more about what he knew of Jesus since he was raised Hindu. He gave a sterile, historic answer that included a couple of details.

I asked him, "Where do you land on this topic?" I wondered if I had been to forceful when he paused again. *Oh, no,* I thought, *not another hour-long pause.* After a few seconds, he said, "I am intrigued about why you keep speaking of Jesus in such a personal way."

I told him that was a great question. Just about that time, the lift jerked and we began to move. I shared briefly about how Jesus was more than a religious figure to me. I told them there was a part of Jesus they might not know much about. I asked if they had ever heard of the Holy Spirit. I suggested they could prayerfully talk directly to Jesus and the Holy Spirit would help them communicate, and I believed they would be pleasantly surprised at the results. By this time, we were ready to off load from the quad. We said how much we enjoyed meeting and talking together and then we parted. It was a conversation that gave me a chance to use my *Christ-encounter story* in a way that opened up a spiritual conversation.

This couple was obviously spiritually open and they were not afraid to discuss spiritual things. The Holy Spirit put me in the right place at the right time. I thanked God for arranging our meeting. I continued to pray that the couple would follow the promptings of the Spirit. This is a case where following the prompting of the Holy Spirit and sharing my *"Christ encounter story"* were major parts of the spiritual conversation that developed that day.

Do you feel your testimony is interesting enough to share? The dramatic testimonies we sometimes wish we had can have unintended consequences. They can de-motivate people to share whose conversion experience isn't a riveting story, which is most of us. The non-dramatic story is in many ways the more powerful story because it is more common experience.

God can use your story even if you don't think it is dramatic. Impressive stories can be entertaining but also completely disconnected from the life of the person with whom you are talking. The goal is not to impress them with a sensational story. The goal is to follow the lead of the Holy Spirit and allow Him to impact their lives.

A Story Based Around a God Truth

The second and most versatile type of testimony is the fusion of God's daily work in our life with the truth in scripture. These stories are essential if to build a discipleship culture. They produce spiritual growth in the disciple and they become powerful, spiritual conversation tools.

Look for how the God of the universe is at work in your day-to-day life. He wants to connect the truth from Scriptures with our daily experiences so we will grow and have confidence that He can lead and direct our lives. This happens when we connect our *story based around a God truth* with a biblical truth God has taught us.

This approach uses brief, strategic stories. They seldom have anything to do with defining your spiritual birth. When talking about ourselves with others, don't we usually talk about what's happening currently? We don't usually start relating the details of our birth years ago. We want mostly to share stories/testimonies regarding what God is currently showing us.

In the book of Revelation, John says the power of Jesus' movement was how followers overcame great opposition "through the blood of the Lamb and the word of their testimony" (Rev. 12:11). We must learn to recognize what God is doing in our lives, and learn to share the stories in a logical way. When we do, we'll find ourselves engaged in significant spiritual conversations that will result in effective disciple making.

How to Connect Scripture with Your Life

When we learn to share our stories wrapped in biblical truth, we are making the Scriptures digestible for a person unfamiliar with them. We share our stories to illustrate the truth of Scriptures. When you identify a potentially disciple-able person be prepared to share your story wrapped in truth they can digest.

This process is what I call learning how to share a milk story/testimony.

"A story is a way to say something that can't be said any other way." -

Flannery O'Connor

Milk Versus Meat

A baby must exclusively consume milk to survive because it doesn't have the digestive system ready to digest complex foods. The necessary gastric juices would eat away at the very soft developing tissue of the fragile infant. Mother's breast milk contains a perfect combination of nutrients to jumpstart this tiny human's first days.

In just a few months, the baby will develop digestive capacities to handle solid food. Before long the baby does not need the same amounts of nutrition from the breast milk because it has developed the ability to eat table food.

Milk is predigested food. It doesn't sound very inviting to think of consuming predigested food, which may be why most adults don't have an appetite for regularly drinking milk except with cereal, or with a warm cookie.

> *Most adults don't find predigested food (milk), very appealing, however babies seem to love it.*

The Apostles Paul and Peter use the metaphor of spiritual milk and spiritual meat to describe how to disciple a new believer. They are talking about how to connect the Good News to people who don't have a digestive system. They say we are to present the Gospel in a milk form for a spiritually young person who can't digest meat.

In the American church we often communicate that milk is bad and meat is good. But the question is not whether milk is good or bad. Milk is necessary. But as a spiritual nutrient it needs to be matched with the proper development stage.

The question is: What is the proper food for the development of the young disciple?" A young disciple who has no capacity to digest complex spiritual truth must be presented truth as if feeding milk to an infant.

Let's review: A milk testimony is a biblical truth that has been digested by you – the disciple maker – and shared with a person who doesn't yet have a spiritual digestive system.

I had the recent opportunity to take a biblical truth and share it in a predigested form. I filtered it through my experience and shared it in a way that could be digested. Instead of quoting the chapter and verse, I simply shared the biblical truth in a testimony.

Here it is: A person turned to me during a conversation among others and asked why I was not spewing a Christian apologetic position. I simply shared that when the conversation becomes intense I like to listen to learn more about why they are so animated. I told the questioner that I had benefitted from scriptural wisdom about listening to understand. I did not quote the passage from James 1:19, about being, "Quick to listen, slow to speak and slow to become angry."

If you're in that situation, you could share a story of how the truth from James 1:19 helps you listen before you speak. In this case I was able to speak to the value of the truth from the Scriptures, without pressing my Christian position.

Utilizing scripture will add weight to your testimony more than simply reciting a Christian teacher. In our current church culture we act like it's effective to share our faith by preaching at people. Do you try to communicate your faith to an unbelievers with a sermonette they can't digest?

You will be more effective with a communication style that includes milk – easily digestible information you've gleaned from scripture, shared through the filter of your life. People are always interested to hear how your life has been changed by the power of God. Used correctly, this fusion of the Holy Spirit, scripture and your story will capture the attention of potential disciples.

When Paul was helping Timothy reflect on his story he said, "I have been reminded of your sincere faith, which first lived in your grandmother Lois and in your mother Eunice and, I am persuaded, now lives in you also" (2 Timothy 1:5). Timothy's conversion story may be the most boring testimony ever written. You may think it sounds like your story.

Maybe you story exchanges the grandmother and mother for a father or a friend, or a coworker or a neighbor. Many testimonies are similar to Timothy's, but he learned to use the power of a milk testimony.

"From infancy you have known the Holy Scriptures, which are able to make you wise for salvation through faith in Christ Jesus," Paul reminds Timothy. "All Scripture is God-breathed and is useful for teaching, rebuking, correcting and training in righteousness, so that the servant of God may be thoroughly equipped for every good work." (2 Timothy 3:15–16)

Earlier, in 2 Timothy 1:14, Paul reminds Timothy that the Holy Spirit is able to guide him, guard him, and make him wise as He makes disciples. The Spirit gives Timothy power to instruct, inspire and correct those he would lead. This still is a gold nugget of discipleship instruction.

It seems that Timothy consumed them in a way that gives him wisdom for coaching his disciples. Timothy was empowered to instruct, inspire, and correct those he would lead. This was, and still is, a gold nugget of discipleship instruction.

Spiritual Sensitivity for Spiritual Conversations

A crusty, retired Marine colonel named Bill started attending our church. Bill had a commanding presence and was obviously hardened by years of service. Still, he was like-able and approachable. I started meeting Bill for coffee to hear his story and determine if he was disciple-able. As I was driving to meet Bill on one of those occasions, the Holy Spirit prompted me to tell Bill, *"God loves you."* I assumed that meant I should share the message of the gospel with him and that I needed to ask if he was ready to respond to Christ as savior. I didn't think much about the prompting, and I proceeded to the meeting.

Bill and I did the classic guy small talk. We discussed sports a bit and then I asked Bill if he had any questions since we'd last met, when I had given him the book *More Than a Carpenter*. This launched us into a conversation that allowed me to share the gospel with Bill. He was asking all the right questions and we were looking to the Scriptures to find the answers.

Bill was learning how to use his Bible. Everything was going well. I asked him where he was in terms of responding to the offer of Jesus in John 1:12. (This is the verse where we are invited to receive Jesus, and believe in His name, and receive the right to become a child of God.) I felt Bill was primed and ready, so I was shocked when he told me he wasn't.

We continued talking for a few more minutes, but Bill seemed to want to wrap it up. As I drove away I was gripped with the idea that I had missed the Holy Spirit's prodding as I was driving to meet Bill. I felt I needed to go back and talk to him again. I fought the prompting to turn around and restart the conversation. I would just wait until next time.

But this feeling was too strong and I turned my car around. Bill was still there. I had no idea how to approach him. Bill looked up and asked me if I forgot something. I felt really awkward. I was ready to say, *"No, I didn't forget something, but I am supposed to ask you again if you want to accept Christ as your Savior."*

Then it hit me—I had forgotten something. I was supposed to tell Bill God loves him. That is what I should have done the first time.

I didn't know what to do but blurt it out. I sighed and said, "Bill, this is weird, but I think that I need to tell you—I paused, almost ashamed of the awkwardness. I swallowed and said, "I think I am supposed to tell you that God really loves you."

He looked shocked. He paused, and then he began to weep— tears ran down his big burly face. He said, "I asked God this morning to prove to me that He loves me." That was what it took, and I would have never seen it. The message seemed so simple and assumed. Of course God loves Bill. How could he not know that? He was now ready to open his life to being a disciple of Jesus. He was ready to take off and grow.

Why was it so urgent that I go back that day? A situation like usually could wait until the next time we were together.

We never did get the chance to engage in the normal process of discipleship. The next week Bill was admitted to the hospital. A couple of weeks later, I stood over his fresh grave and told the story of how God had demonstrated His love to Bill.

I told those gathered how the Spirit had so capably prompted me with the exact words to say. I shared how clumsily I had botched the process at first and how the Spirit turned me around. It was a powerful reminder that God will lead us in amazing ways if we will listen to the promptings of His Spirit.

The foundation for making disciples is developing the skill of learning to listen to the voice of the Holy Spirit, and responding to Him.

Yet, learning to listen to the Holy Spirit is foreign to most Christ followers. We haven't been trained to hear and discern the voice of God, or how to respond to it. Jesus is our example of how a leader establishes a new culture and language.

Jesus introduced the idea that His disciples would be serving in a "new kingdom culture." Everything Jesus taught, every story He told, every action He took was wrapped in the language of this new Kingdom. Jesus used the Old Testament Jewish culture as His launching point and He rolled out the language and philosophy of the new Kingdom in the Sermon on the Mount.

To create a culture of reproducing disciples, Jesus centered His teaching around learning to have spiritual conversations. Disciples would learn to ask questions and to use testimonies to share information.

This was a new culture and a new way of thinking. Jesus was not creating an institution or a structure, but making sure that everything he was communicating was simple and reproducible for the common person.

He didn't want His disciples to preach at people. Preaching is one-way communication that has become offensive in our culture. All preaching does is provide biblical information. People will not embrace the life-changing message of the gospel if they don't discover if for themselves. The Soviet psychologist, and founder of a theory of human cultural and bio-social development, Lev Vygotsky said, "Oral language is the primary way humans process ideas."

Just hearing an idea doesn't mean we will understand it. We are not able to embrace or fully understand an idea until we are able to speak it. One-way communication is not an effective gateway for learning. Change requires a dialogue.

When we cultivate spiritual conversations, we apply the softer, more personal communication that Jesus used. Jesus' way of sharing information connected with the perspective of the potential disciple.

Changing Our Approach

In the past, we trained people to debate and argue with those whose opinions differed from ours. This is called *apologetics*. We believed that we must debate all people who hold an opposing view or we are not doing our duty as card-carrying Christians. Christians felt pressure not to let God down, so we locked horns with scoffers and skeptics.

This approach produced more scoffers and skeptics.

It's like trying to rid your yard of dandelions. The more you pull at them the more you send their fragile seeds airborne. Trying to remove dandelions spreads the seeds, thus creating a yard full of weeds.

In the early 2000s, I co-authored a book that was intended to be an apologetic work. We wanted to answer the 40 top questions people have related to God. Our motivation was to equip Christians with the tools they needed to defend the Christian position when skeptics and scoffers pushed against them. It's called *The God Questions*.

As we wrote the book, we shifted our approach. I became more convinced that when you win doctrinal, theological and apologetic arguments, your debate opponent tends to move farther from God, and double down on his position.

So, we took a different approach and aimed the book at helping Christ followers know how to build a solid basis for their beliefs so they could confidently love God and those He placed in their lives. It became more about giving Christ followers the confidence to truly become a disciple – to know Christ and understand the truth that is their basis for believing. When they took this step, they began to love people like Jesus did, instead of trying to win debates.

In the book *Blue Like Jazz,* author Donald Miller went through a process of changing how he approached those far from Christ. He shares a spiritual conversation he had with a talk-show host who was hostile to Christianity. The host attempted to draw Miller into a confrontation on the air:

> *He asked me if I was a Christian, and I told him yes.*
> *"Why don't you want to defend Christianity?" He*
> *acted confused. I told him I no longer knew what*

the term meant. Of the hundreds of thousands of
people listening to his show that day, some of them
had terrible experiences with Christianity; they
may have been yelled at by a teacher in a Christian
school, abused by a minister, or browbeaten by a
Christian parent. To them, the term Christianity
meant something that no Christian I know would
defend. By fortifying the term, I am only making
them more and more angry. I won't do it. Stop ten
people on the street and ask them what they think of
when they hear the word Christianity, and they will
give you ten different answers. How can I define the
term that means ten different things to ten different
people? I told the radio-show host that I would
rather talk about Jesus, and how I came to believe
that Jesus exists and that He likes me. The host
looked back at me with tears in his eyes. When we
were done, he asked if we could go get lunch togeth-
er. He spoke of how he had always wanted to be-
lieve that Jesus was the son of God.[14]

In this exchange, Miller demonstrates how to connect with a person who processes the world differently. Likewise, we will encounter many who are ready to debate us or resist us. If we engage them without asking questions, we'll never make any
progress. The word *Christian* has been so convoluted and assigned so many definitions by those inside and outside the faith

---

[14] Donald Miller, *Blue Like Jazz*, (Nashville: Thomas Nelson, 2003), p.115.

that we can never move to disciple a person if we our starting point is "being Christian."

Most of my productive discipleship relationships began when they pushed back or objected to Christianity. At least they cared enough to push back. If a person is apathetic, there is little you can do to engage them. The person pushing back cares enough to resist.

> *Resistance can be a sign of potential disciple-ability. It may reveal that they care enough to argue with you. Apathetic people are completely un-discpleable. Too many church members are often apathetic, and therefore they are not disciple-able.*

How many people in your church do you think would be difficult to disciple because they are spiritually apathetic? They've passed a short test that stamps them "Christian," but for the most part don't consider there is anything more to it.

One of my neighbors in California was a trial attorney named James. He attended our church for several years, but resisted being baptized, or formally giving his life to Christ. I spent hours in spiritual conversations with James. He interacted with me about my sermons and fully embraced our direction. One day I asked him why he was so reluctant to give his life to Christ. He said:

> *I already trust God more than most in your church who call themselves Christ followers. It seems that*

*most of the people in the church who say they are
Christ followers have little interest in really following
Jesus, or really loving Him... I don't understand why
a person would want to go to the effort of being la-
beled a Christian and not really be one.*

I had to admit he was right. This man – on the path to becoming
a disciple – was distracted by others who merely called themselves Christ followers. James never publicly formalized his relationship with Jesus, but he did become a disciple and made an
impact with his life.

James and I began our discipleship journey as he faced jail time
for engaging in criminal activity with a client he represented. He
was a broken man, eager to learn more about Jesus and open to
becoming a disciple. If I ever mentioned the church, he wanted
no part of that conversation. But the more I shared of my personal encounter with Jesus and how it had changed my life, the
more he was interested. I wanted James to see Jesus for who He
is and not through his cultural Christian misunderstanding.

During this season, I learned to speak *of* Jesus, not just talk
about Jesus. This proved to be a major lesson in learning to
make disciples.

What's the difference in those prepositions "of" and "about?" We
can spout off the ideas of others we don't really believe. We do it
all the time. The atheist who says he doesn't believe in God often
is just replaying a statement he's heard before. These people are
not much different from the church person who repeats an idea

they heard in a sermon. You can speak *about* Jesus, but not really know Him.

When someone speaks of Jesus in a personal way, it is startling. You may never have heard a person speak that way. It cuts through defenses. This is a level of familiarity we can achieve only by being open to the person of the Holy Spirit. He enables us to speak of Jesus and not simply about Him.

It's easy to talk about Christianity as a theory without making the conversation personal. When you talk about who Jesus is to you, you move the conversation from historic and theoretical to current and personal.

There is no way I can speak of Jesus in an impersonal manner. When we come to know Jesus, our speech gets stripped of its religiosity and we simply focus on who Jesus is as a person. This changes the way we think about Him – and the way we speak about Him.

This approach reduces the need for apologetics. We don't need to debate about Jesus, because we are not trying to argue a point. We can simply tell our story and expect the Holy Spirit to use the story to direct the conversation, like the woman at the well in the book of John. After she met Jesus, she told the townspeople, "Come and see for yourself."

It is a simple invitation. This approach may open our eyes to the possibility we're preaching the wrong message. We should not be trying to get nonbelievers to think and vote like we do. There is limited value in persuading resistant people to come to our church services or special events.

Jesus didn't start with gaining agreement on a set of beliefs. Carl Medearis says, "Here in the West, reason is king. We have doctrines and apologetics and really nifty devices to solidify the right thoughts. If it doesn't make sense, it's not relevant."[15]

We must learn to value a different set of outcomes. If we will value spiritual conversations that center on Jesus, the result will be discipleship relationships. We will see disciples reproduce disciples. If we continue to talk to people about church services and programs, we will continue to get sterile non-reproducing disciples.

The four Gospels are essential to learning to speak of Jesus. Reading the Gospels will introduce you to the person of Jesus. This is different from simply being familiar with Him. I suggest that you consume the person of Jesus if you want to make disciples and use your life to make an impact.

The Art of Asking Questions

Asking questions is your primary tool for effective spiritual conversations. Learning to ask good questions will allow the Holy Spirit to lead you to connect with people who think and engage differently than you.

---

[15] Medearis, Carl, Speaking of Jesus: The Art of Not-Evangelism Colorado Springs, David C. Cook. p. 48.

It's a learned skill that Jesus demonstrated. He almost always posed a question at some point in a conversation. We see this skill at work as Jesus interacted with the three groups that surrounded Him in the first century. The first group was the religious legalists who opposed Him and wanted Him dead. The second group was those who had been ostracized from the religious community. They were described by Jesus as "sheep without a shepherd" (Matthew 9:36). The third group were those Jesus was developing as followers.

Jesus used 233 questions to set the direction for His discipling culture.

Even though each group was different, He asked questions among them all. Jesus' questions revealed their values and priorities. He perfected the art of setting direction by asking questions.

I am confident Jesus was known for how closely He listened. The first step in developing effective spiritual conversations is learning to listen to the person and the Holy Spirit at the same time so you can form the right question. When we listen and ask questions we build a bridge. If a topic comes up that causes spiritual tension, asking the right question can produce discipleship traction.

When I hung out with my friends from the radio station, I was genuinely curious why the other on-air personalities were resistant to the church and Jesus. I had never met such a resistant group. I met plenty of people who were apathetic or had other belief systems. But this group positively was resistant. The only way to build a bridge to these guys was by asking questions. Radio personalities are happy to give you their opinions.

As I showed interest in learning more about their world views, they became less combative and more eager to share. Most of the on-air personalities had some experience with church people. It was church people who turned them away from Jesus. They found Christians narrow minded and judgmental.

Apologetics are designed to assist people who are struggling to embrace a Biblical world view. They are not effective in the early stages of spiritual conversations.

Some of them had been rejected by church people. In all cases, there was some measure of pain in their processes. I didn't try to defend the Church or the behavior of Christians. I just wanted to talk about Jesus. As a result, it wasn't long before they did as well.

DEVELOPING A
HUNGER FOR THE SCRIPTURES

I usually leave a spiritual conversation inspired to open scripture and learn more about the biblical worldview of whatever topic we just discussed. Spiritual conversations almost always raise tough topics and questions and I enjoy wrestling with them. Spiritual conversations naturally create tensions that drive me to look to scripture for answers.

The Starfish movement will not gain traction if our goal is to win arguments with those we are trying to reach. Jesus sent His disciples to look for "persons of peace" in the villages around north Galilee. They embarked on this mission with little information and no Bible in hand, armed only with their spiritual conversation skills and the power of the Holy Spirit.

THE FUEL FOR DISCIPLES

In the New Testament there are two words for time: *kairos* and *chronos*. We still use the root of those words today. We have a device called a chronometer, but most of us call it a watch. We use words like chronological and anachronism. *Chronos* refers to the measure of clock time such as seconds, minutes, hours and years.

Kairos is qualitative. It measures what God can do in a moment, not seconds. Further, it refers to the opportune moment. God's timing is not measured in seconds but by events and providential encounters. Perhaps it's a moment when everything changes. In a *kairos* moment the eternal God breaks into your circumstances. In *kairos* moments, the measure of *chronos* time seems to be suspended.

We've all had major life-change *kairos* moments. Do you remember your graduation, your marriage, the birth of your children? These are all *kairos* moments, a moment when time stands still. *Kairos* moments leave an impact, but not all come in a dramatic wrapper. They can be the gnawing unrest of a successful 45-year old going through a midlife transition. It can be a mom who identified herself through her kids, but who is now figuring out the next stage of her life. When you learn to recognize *kairos* moments you'll see that disciple-able people are those wrestling with the *Kairos,* not the *chronos.*

When a person is at this disciple-able moment, he or she can seldom identify it. They can't tell you what is going on with them. They often come asking a God-based question. How we handle this exchange makes all the difference.

> *Discipleship tension often emerges in the form of a challenging question. Don't miss the kairos moment that may be wrapped in a tough question.*

If we do what most of us were trained to do, we will miss this *kairos* moment. Most of us were trained to provide a specific answer when asked a God-based question. That's how we were trained in Bible college or seminary. It is natural to kick into "Bible answer-man mode." But when we offer a theological answer, we are not following the Jesus model.

Jesus knew how to look beyond the question to find the motivation. Until we explore we cannot know how to respond properly. This approach requires most of our pastors and leaders to detox. We must change how we think about our role and response and resist the urge to answer a question and move on. Some call that pastoral ministry. However, it isn't what Jesus did or what He is calling us to do.

As long as we keep feeling we need to answer people's questions, we will struggle to identify disciple-able people. We will also miss the opportunity to help them look to the Scriptures to find the answers for themselves. Jesus knew every question has the potential to open up a discipling conversation. If we offer a quick answer we miss what lies behind the question.

I encourage you to take a different approach. When people come searching for information encourage them to ask questions so you can discover why they're searching. Don't discourage genuine curiosity by providing an easy answer.

Instead, ask if they would be willing to find the information in the Scriptures for themselves with your guidance. This approach will equip and enable people to search the Scriptures on their own and become less dependent on you.

1. The best thing that can happen to a new follower of Jesus is to learn how to have effective spiritual conversations.

2. When they take this step they will encounter hard questions. Teach them it's okay to face questions they can't answer.

3. You will have a better exchange if you affirm the question and then ask if they want to look to the Scriptures to find the answer. You will create a discipling relationship because the tension that this produces can be a

great motivator for this new disciple to immerse himself into the Scriptures for answers.

The average Christian has been flooded with teaching and sermons. This ocean of teaching excess actually has the opposite effect of what was intended. Instead of making the listener more confident, the church member feels inadequate to communicate on his or her own. If they can't communicate like the teacher, they remain silent. The result is our spiritual conversations sound like sermons and the average person feels inadequate to engage in an information-intensive debate with a person far from God.

Too many Christ followers have become convinced that they can't share their faith unless they can communicate a skillful message complete with memorized Biblical references.

This misunderstanding creates a barrier to real discipleship. There were no professional communicators in the early church teaching an abundance of "just in case" information. There were only rookie followers sharing their stories in a simple, personal way.

It is essential that we teach new disciples not to feel the pressure to answer people's questions. Instead, we must show them how to let spiritual conversations drive the disciple-able person to find his or her own answers in the Scriptures. This is the tension that can motivate them to explore and learn the Scriptures for themselves.

When a person begins the process of making disciples, we encourage them to purchase a couple of tools. They need a reference Bible; they don't need a study Bible. A reference tool can be a phone app, a computer software solution, or a reference Bible such as the *Thompson Chain Reference Bible.*

There is a difference between a study Bible and a reference Bible. A study Bible often gives preprocessed answers from the author. Many authors have released their own study Bibles, as if they wrote it themselves. What they have done is load the pages with notes from past sermons. A reference Bible assists the disciple to discover the answer on his or her own. When a person learns how to search for topics in the Bible they will discover a hunger for the power of God's truth in Scriptures. Help them select the tool that is best for them.

Church leaders are frustrated that attendees have little hunger to search the Scriptures for truth on which to build their lives. What would it be like if the majority of those in church were passionately hungry for the Scriptures? What if they regularly discussed ways to live life based on the Scriptures?

This happens when a disciple is shown how to search the Scriptures for answers to his or her own questions. No curriculum will produce a disciple who can search the Scriptures and build a biblical worldview.

Knowing Jesus is Different From Knowing About Jesus

We've become accustomed to believing that knowing about something is the same thing as knowing something.

We have managed to teach people about God. We teach them about prayer. We teach them how to thrive in our program-centered church environments. Making disciples isn't teaching people to just know about Christ and the Christian life. Spiritual conversations based on disciple-making will set the focus on actually knowing Jesus.

In Matthew 7:21 Jesus reminds us, "Not everyone who says to me, 'Lord, Lord,' will enter the kingdom of heaven, but only the one who does the will of my Father..." It's not enough just to know about Jesus. We must know Him personally. We can help others find Him as we share how He has changed us. God uses spiritual conversations to bring about real change in a disciple's life.

The existing model tries to persuade others to have a relationship with Jesus based on information we share about Jesus. Then, we try to improve behavior by teaching Bible morality lessons and Bible character information.

Instead, Jesus invited us to know Him in the most personal kind of way. He gave an illustration of a vine and branch in John 15. We are invited to receive our life source from Jesus, to grow in Him and to reproduce the same fruit He produces. If we are to know Jesus in a personal and intimate way we must move beyond merely learning information about Him.

Sports fans absorb trivia and facts about their favorite teams or players. A person obsessed with a celebrity will learn everything they can about that person. Becoming a disciple is more than gathering Jesus trivia and knowing Bible facts. The result of a vibrant and intimate relationship is actually allowing your life to grow out of the person-ness of Jesus.

If you are married you probably had a season where you were deliriously smitten. In that phase you hungered to know every scintilla of information you could about your new love, no matter how trivial. As the relationship grew, you probably moved on to a place where you knew him or her so well that you could finish their sentences. You knew how he thought. You became so familiar that you could operate in unison.

Knowing Jesus intellectually is nowhere close to the same as knowing Jesus intimately. That's why in Philippians 3:10 Paul cried out, "I want to know Christ and the power of His resurrection and the fellowship of sharing in the sufferings." He already knew all the data about Jesus. Paul is inviting us to join him on the journey to grow as a disciple.

Settling for information about Jesus without knowing Him personally produces an impotent life and a powerless church. It also produces a false confidence in followers who base their assurances on the level of information they have acquired.

Leaders loaded with information, but whose lives are not changing to become like Jesus often become NBAs (Non-Bought-in Adversaries). When our leadership metrics get twisted we produce leaders who know church but don't know Jesus.

In the New Testament, elders were leaders who shared the impact Jesus made on them. Before long they were leading discipleship movements. Paul never seemed to care how much Bible trivia they knew. In Titus 1 and 1 Timothy 3, Paul says nothing about biblical knowledge being required to oversee a church movement. Everything about leadership in those passages has to do with allowing the Spirit of God to make such substantive changes.

There was no place in the New Testament church for positional leadership. A positional leader is someone who holds a leadership position, but who hasn't produced any spiritual fruit, or reproduced disciples. Today we have pastors and elders who hold those positions because they learned the right information, passed tests, and satisfied ordination councils. Positional leadership almost always emerges from a church with no multiplication culture.

We seldom take into account what Paul told Titus. The leader "must hold firmly to the trustworthy messages as it has been taught, so he can encourage others by sound doctrine..." (Titus 1:9).

The word *doctrine* is the Greek word *didaskalia*. It means to teach and instruct concepts or precepts. The concepts or precepts

Jesus taught all related to loving and knowing the Father through the Son. From that relational position we are to follow the Spirit as He leads us to go and make disciples.

Most churches operate under a set of doctrinal positions designed to keep the church theologically focused. That is a very important point. We lose our way when we think that teaching church doctrine is discipleship. Doctrines are guardrails for the church at large to keep it from running off the track.

But, knowing doctrine instead of knowing Jesus will produce spiritual death. We must establish a culture that focuses on discipleship reproduction.

CHAPTER 8

IDENTIFY A
PERSON OF PEACE

PRINCIPLE TWO

At the midway point of His three-year public ministry, Jesus seems to shift His approach radically. In the first 18 months we see Jesus focusing all of His attention on His 12 disciples in the northern region of the Sea of Galilee. During this time He teaches and performs a few miracles, and occasionally speaks to the crowds, but He mostly spends time in smaller gatherings.

Then suddenly it seems that Jesus shifts to a new phase with His disciples that changes everything for them. Jesus sent them out in pairs, not as a group. They returned to the region where He had taken them repeatedly with very basic instructions to proclaim the "Kingdom of God, and to heal the sick." They were to take nothing for the journey—no staff, no bag, no bread, no money, no extra shirt. In Luke 9:4–6, He instructed them:

> "Whatever house you enter, stay there until you leave that town. If people do not welcome you, leave their town and shake the dust off your feet as a testimony against them." So they set out and went from village to village, proclaiming the good news and healing people everywhere.

Jesus made a point to tell them that if they were not received well, they shouldn't take the rejection personally. He emphasized that the purpose of this mission was to find and establish a relationship with a "person of peace." This would become the foundational principle for kingdom expansion throughout the remainder of the New Testament. In Luke 10:5–7, Jesus established this approach:

> "When you enter a house first say, 'Peace be to this house.' If a man of peace is there, your peace will rest on him; but if not, it will return to you. Stay in that house... Do not move around from house to house."

The person of peace is the one who leads or influences a group of people. In the Bible the word is *household*. The Greek term for this group of people is *oikos*. We will discuss this concept more in the next chapter. The instructions are clear. The disciple-maker pairs were to keep moving until they found a receptive person. When they did, they were to stay in that household. Jesus was saying discipleship can't come from superficial relationships; it only happens when we invest in the right people.

Jesus calls a disciple-able person, a "person of peace." The Greek word *eirene,* (translated as *peace*) has to do with finding a person who is not fighting with God. In other words, a person who is receptive to the way of peace the Messiah brings, someone spiritually open to the work of the Spirit of God in his or her life. Finding this person is the critical first step to launching a starfish movement.

These instructions were given with a purpose, so the disciples could experience the tension necessary for them to grow as obedient followers. They needed to fully engage with Jesus' mission, and learn to trust that Jesus had led them well. They would have to depend upon the leading of the Spirit in all they did. Jesus immersed them in one of the most intense, growth promoting experiences possible.

This experience would be like you and I being told one day to get on a bus, destination unknown. Leave your cell phone, wallet and computer behind. Take no money and no second set of clothes. Were we brave or naive enough to step onto the bus, we'd be driven to an unfamiliar village and disgorged to fend for ourselves with the simple instruction to find a person open to the things of God.

Our goal is to reproduce what we had gleaned from our time with Jesus, so we could try to launch a movement the way He had. This season of reinforcement was critical to the disciples. Jesus didn't want His guys to go very long without applying what He had taught them. They were thrust into a situation where they had to reproduce the culture that Jesus had given them.

Jesus taught the disciples to look for others who were drawn by the Father. Jesus taught us that the Father would place a desire in us to pursue Him. In John 6:44 He said, "No one can come to me unless the Father draws them."

Jesus gave us a new standard for measuring our success. Instead of measuring converts, we should measure discipleship progress. That doesn't jive with the budgets, buildings and butts in the pews culture today. He said, "Do not rejoice that the spirits submit to you, but rejoice that your names are written in heaven" (Luke 10:20).

Jesus' words in verse 20 are rather startling, reminding the disciples who were naturally wowed by their victories over demonic forces, that they should celebrate the bigger picture because their names are written in heaven.

In our US churches, we assure people of salvation when they mouth the formulaic "sinner's prayer." We almost infer that reciting such a "magic formula" reserves for them a place in eternity. We tell people they are to rejoice that their names are written in heaven sooner than Jesus did.

Jesus told His disciples they are assured of Kingdom life only when they decide to live in a Kingdom fashion. The measure of this assurance would be disciples who reproduced disciples.

It's God's Kingdom advance that causes "Satan to fall like lightning from the sky." Yet US churches continue to emphasize outward behaviors. These behaviors are associated with acting like a Christian, such as being baptized, repeating a catechism, or saying a "sinners prayer." Instead, Jesus focused on launching a culture of reproduction.

I was leading training in Philadelphia when an engineer named Todd asked me if I'd noticed the pattern that emerged in what I was teaching about the disciples going out two by two, looking for persons of peace. I had to admit that I hadn't. He said, "Jesus divided the 12 into six pairs of two, right? If you multiply 6 x 12 you get 72. The seventy-two were mostly brought by the disciples to meet Jesus and to connect with the larger group of disciples, right?"

> "After this the Lord appointed the seventy-two and sent them two by two ahead of him to every town and place where he was about to go" (Luke 10:1).

Yes, that's correct. It seems Jesus quickly sent out the 72 to continue the process of reproduction.

"Next, the seventy-two were sent out in pairs," Todd said. "They went out and did the same thing the 12 did, right?"

I agreed, and he went on, "If you notice, every level of multiplication happens when Jesus sends out pairs of disciples who return with a small *ekklesia* of twelve total. If you take the 72 He sent out and multiply them by 12, you have the next growth point.

"The 72 were sent out in 36 pairs, right?" If you multiply 36 x 12 you get 500." The next major numeric jump occurred in 1 Corinthians 15:6, where it says: "After that, he appeared to more than five hundred of the brothers and sisters at the same time, most of whom are still living."

"After Jesus was resurrected and the next multiplication ripple is reported, the 500 multiply to 3,000," Todd said. "Again, if you take 500 and divide it in half, and then multiply the 250 pairs by 12, the number is 3,000."

I told him that is also correct. In Acts 2:41 it says: "Those who accepted His message were baptized, and about three thousand were added to their number that day."

Todd's voice rose and he asked me about the final measurable marker we have in scripture. He reminded me I had said that the 5,000 referenced in Acts 4:4 was likely only the number of men. A crowd of men that size could swell as high as 18,000 were you to count women and children. The book of Acts records: "But many who heard the message believed; so the number of men who believed grew to about five thousand" (Acts 4:4).

"Again," Todd said, keeping his principle consistent, "if you take 3,000 people and place them into pairs, and then multiply the 1,500 pairs by 12 you get 18,000. The Bible doesn't give us any more numbers to analyze like this."

Todd was right. A clear pattern had emerged in the starfish movement Jesus launched. We don't have the specifics of how the last several ripples happened, but it was apparent that Jesus started a culture that rippled outward without need of much oversight. The disciples were reproducing what they had experienced. Note that immediately after His resurrection, when Jesus appeared to His followers on the road to Emmaus, they were traveling in pairs.

I'm not saying it happened in a precise way, such as pairs of disciples finding people of peace, and soon there was an *ekklesia* of 12 disciples gathered. I'm just saying the culture Jesus launched obviously rippled out in a way that stayed true to the way that it began.

Often we credit a sudden appearance of the Holy Spirit for the 3,000 who were "added to their number on the day of Pentecost." But, it's not like the Spirit of God had been asleep in a corner of heaven and the Father woke Him to show up for His grand entrance on the day of Pentecost. He had been around from the beginning, hovering over the creation in Genesis 1.

The dramatic explosion of followers came at Pentecost not because the Holy Spirit suddenly showed up, but because Jesus had cleared a path to the Father through the cross. He also launched a starfish culture of disciple making that could ripple through time. The combination of Holy Spirit power and Jesus' starfish movement created the Pentecost expansion that multiplied believers around the world.

These principles form the core foundation for developing disciples who will grow to lead other disciples. They are tools to usher in the work of the Kingdom with those hungry to pursue a transformed life in Christ.

We can't advance the Kingdom of God without the discipleship strategy Jesus gave us. He invites us to partner with Him as we discover the ways God's Spirit is stirring in us.

Paul, who wrote 60 percent of the New Testament, taught new followers how to grow as disciples. He describes the process as learning to walk differently.

In Galatians 5:25, he describes it like this: "We live by the Spirit, let us keep in step with the Spirit." He encourages us to keep in step with the promptings and lead of our disciple making coach, the Holy Spirit.

CHAPTER 9

Teach Them to Reach their Oikos

PRINCIPLE THREE

When movie studio boss, Harry Flugleman, explained to his characters in *The Three Amigos* why their last few movies had been box office flops, he said, in no uncertain terms, "We strayed from the formula and we paid the price!"

What's not so funny is that the Church has done the same thing by unwittingly and gradually allowing Jesus' formula for building His Church to fade into the background. We've relegated His mission to reach those who are far from Christ to some kind of optional church program, and we've paid a very dear and eternal price.[16]

Tragically, many Christ followers will wake up one day to realize they wasted their best season of relational impact. While the Church has used guilt, pressure and programs to get young families to join the institution, if we had followed Jesus' model, we could have harnessed this powerful group to launch starfish movements of disciples.

One season of your life is more potent than others for teaching and learning. I call it the sticky years. It's the season around the years you raise your children. This season can literally be sticky. It's a busy and chaotic season at times, but also a rich time of connectedness and high-impact community life.

By the time your children are in high school, you discover your high-impact relational communities are starting to shrink. As parents enter the empty-nest years, it is harder to connect with a high-impact group. The sad truth is that most aging adults will find themselves disconnected from any high-impact community other than their families.

In the Bible the Greek word *oikos* refers to these high-impact communities. From this point on, I will refer to these high-impact communities as *oikos*. Tom Mercer shares this insight from a missionary in his book *Eight to Fifteen*:

---

[16]Mercer, Tom 8 to 15, The World Is Smaller Than You Think, Oikos Books.p 45

"A missionary from Bangladesh shares that he failed to take the principle of the high-impact community seriously. He confesses, 'Our individualistic Western thinking led us to a style of outreach termed 'extractionist.' That is, it disregarded the inquirer's *oikos* and even viewed it as a barrier rather than a gift from God! So, we ripped a new believer from their *oikos*... Then we wondered why they were unable to reach out to anyone with the Good News... We then had to provide him/her with a new *oikos*, almost always made up entirely of people who were already Christians... We wondered why it seemed they could reach almost no one, no matter how profound their salvation experience."[17]

We put most adult converts through this same experience when they come into the local church. Our well-intentioned desire to help them grow as Christians by isolating them from their past, sinful environment has the unintended consequence of isolating them from their *oikos* who they could disciple. This actually stunts their growth as new Christ followers.

In human development, a baby will never develop immunity to disease if they are isolated in a sterile environment and never exposed to bacteria. We are designed to grow best when we learn to grow disciples out of our old *oikos*.

---

[17] Ibid. p 55

Of course, the new Christ follower needs the encouragement of a Christian community. They need both their new family of Christ followers and their past *oikos*. The two work in tandem. New followers will have their eyes opened to things that they never noticed before and will see their *oikos* differently. Jesus explained in John 3:3, "No one can see the kingdom of God unless they are born again." They need the help from their new *oikos*, the *ekklesia*/church to help them make disciples from their old *oikos*.

Are you frustrated that you weren't taught how to cultivate disciples like Jesus did? Our hearts desire to do Jesus asks in the Great Commission. We all dream of making our lives pleasing to Jesus by making disciples who reproduce disciples. In Matthew 16:8, Jesus tells us not to put effort into "building the church" because that is His job. He made it very clear in Matthew 28:19 that our job is to "make disciples." In fact, Jesus only mentions the translated word for church twice in the Gospels. It is clear He gave us His plan: to "make disciples," and then He will "build the church."

Mainline denominations are trying frantically to plant churches. Even though Jesus told us our focus should be on making disciples, denominations are focused on establishing institutional churches instead. Their motivation comes from the serious decline of their brands. Their church-planting efforts will not produce the results they desire and there is no possibility they will unleash movements. At best, these churches will last a few years and then become irrelevant as the culture continues to change rapidly. Churches that focus on disciple making will flourish, while attempts to rescue the Church through church planting will fade or fail.

Everyone Wants
A Circle of Friends

Were you among tens of millions who tuned in each week from 1994 to 2004 to see what would happen next in a Manhattan *oikos* that formed around a coffee shop called the Central Perk? The TV show *Friends* drew millions of fans because each of us wants a close circle of friends. Remember, the classic Greek definition of *oikos* means circle of influence, which is often translated to mean household.

We long to be integral in a network of relationships that come together for a common purpose. Without an *oikos* we feel isolated and alone. Our relationships give our lives meaning and value. God wants to add value by leading us to live and connect in community.

Building an *oikos* fits into our natural lifestyle rhythm because it's organic. It's totally authentic—there is nothing programmatic about it. You don't have to create it because it is already at work wherever you live, work, and play. It fits all ages and stages of life; it transcends adulthood. *Oikos*-Based discipleship will work among teens, young adults, and mature adults. It even works in children's ministry. It emerges naturally because the model is so simple.

At one of our Generate Intensive training events a couple from near Washington, DC, was going through the exercises, and the wife became increasingly animated. During a break, she announced that she knew how to do this "*oikos* thing." For her, it was a breakthrough moment.

She said that before, whenever the topic of making disciples came up, she felt like a failure as a Christian. She admitted this issue was keeping her from fully embracing her husband's call to be a church planter. The strategy of reaching the people in her *oikos*/relationship circle fit the way that she was made.

Jesus was brilliant when He launched His Church/*ekklesia* because he built a movement that coincides with something that each of us is already a part of. It shows we can make disciples using our own natural inclinations.

Each of us is part of a group of people whom God has supernaturally and strategically placed in our relational worlds. He did this so we could show them His love. Jesus designed, modeled and taught the *oikos* principle for one purpose: to launch disciples who would change the world.

In the previous chapter we saw how Jesus launched His movement through the "person of peace." He was teaching His followers to identify an existing *oikos* leader. Jesus knew the leader is the primary person empowered to invite someone to join the *oikos*. He sent His guys to the surrounding villages so they could learn to find a "person of peace" and influence them and their *oikos*. We don't know how long they spent in the surrounding towns and villages, likely a few months since it had to be long enough for them to connect with an existing *oikos*.

They didn't need a lot of skill, they needed just enough training to attract and lead a group of 12. From this point, *ekklesia/* churches would be built around cultivating *oikos* relationships. The Roman world had grown to more than 62 million and extended into Europe, Africa and Asia. By 313, the starfish movement had grown to approximately 30 million Christ followers who were meeting in *oikos*-based *ekklesia/*churches.[18] The starfish movement was embraced by nearly half of the Roman world.

Most of the time an *oikos* is a collection of three or four families. It might be a collection of five to 14 individuals who connect apart from their families, but an *oikos* seldom varies past those numbers. Groups of that size can form close communities. Sometimes they can be known as a social clique. We've known such *oikos* from first grade. It doesn't take long for us to do what is natural to us.

We long to gather in small groups of close friends; it is foundational to the human experience. Every culture and people group naturally forms *oikos* groups. It is the foundational unit of society, and it's how we have survived throughout history.

The benefit of *oikos* is that they are resilient and relatively easy to maintain. When we learn how to cultivate an *oikos*, we learn

---

[18]Wikipedia, Constatine the Great and Christianity, January 2013.

how to make disciples in a more natural way. It removes much of the weird factor that has been associated with "doing evangelism" because the relationships are so organic.

Building a starfish culture has a lot to do with cultivating previously formed *oikos* relationships and transforming them for the Kingdom. An *oikos* that is reached has tentacles that spread into multiple other *oikos* groups. When you get permission to join an *oikos*, you are invited to help shape the culture.

Jesus and the Apostle Paul both used a similar strategy to expand the *ekklesia*/church by focusing on developing a healthy *oikos* community. Jesus told His followers to search for receptivity. When they found it, they were to stay and cultivate the relationships that came from that *oikos*. During the short season they were on mission, Jesus wanted them to cultivate one group as deeply as possible.

We don't know how Jesus called His disciples back to the home base in Capernaum when their mission was finished, but they seemed to return at an appointed time. There is something powerful about giving people a set amount of time to accomplish a task. With no time limit there is no sense of urgency. The disciples knew the time was short. They had to get after it, or they would not complete their missions.

When we launch a discipleship culture we give our disciples two-weeks to find discipleable people. We bring them back together and ask them to share what God has been doing in that season.

Keeping people accountable reinforces the new disciple-making culture.

In the New Testament communal culture, an *oikos* was a small village. Members of these tight knit communities depended on each other to stay alive. When we focus on disciple making in an *oikos*, life change happens not in a vacuum, but among people in a group who know you, and who have examined your life. *Oikos*-based groups produce a fresh level of honesty. You can't fake it with people who really know you. The *oikos* helps you merge your Christian life with your existing relationships where you can cultivate potential disciples.

Reaching your social group can have huge impact. On the other hand, reaching your immediate family members may provide the least amount of discipleship traction. They may dismiss the changes in your life because they have seen you go through changes before and think "this Jesus thing" is a passing fad. Jesus said in Matthew 13:57:

> "A prophet is not without honor except in his own town and in his own family (*oikos*). And He did not do many miracles there because of their lack of faith."

Over and over Jesus intentionally demonstrates building His discipleship culture as an *oikos*-centered movement. After healing the demon possessed man in Mark 5:19, Jesus told him to: "Go to your own people [*oikos*] and tell them how much the Lord has done for you." Jesus was instructing the healed man to process his miracle through the relationships in his *oikos*. By doing that, others eventually would follow Jesus.

When Jesus invited Matthew to "follow me," Matthew immediately gave Jesus access to his *oikos*. In another setting, Jesus recognizes Zacchaeus and quickly includes his *oikos*. Jesus said, "Today salvation has come to this house [*oikos*]" (Luke 19:8).

Our *oikos* environments always have been the context where we have the greatest influence. Each of us is part of a natural gathering of people who come together for a variety of reasons. In most cases there is a mix of individuals who know Jesus, or have been exposed to Him or who just have a poor picture of who He is.

I recommend using the same discipleship strategy. You gain momentum when you can launch your discipleship culture out of existing relationships. The unique quality of *oikos*-based groups that emerge from the starfish culture is that they form out of natural relationship patterns. They do not require an outside agent to establish, maintain and prop them up. They form with a high degree of relational "glue" to hold them together. They have no need to focus on a central leader or common weekend experience to cement a relational bond. Groups have bandwidth to focus on discipleship making if they are established with starfish multiplication DNA.

WHO IS THE HOLY SPIRIT DEALING WITH?

I remember it like it was yesterday. I saved for six months to fund my trip to the evangelism super conference near Santa Fe, New Mexico. It had speakers from all over the world.

One speaker prompted us to develop a heart for those who were far from Christ. He encouraged us to write down the names of five people we would share Christ with when we returned home. I remember I was so excited to share Jesus with my friends. I was motivated and ready to see the exciting results of my new-found motivation. When I returned home, I boldly "witnessed" to those whose names I'd written down. Nobody responded and I quickly abandoned the list and lost the fervor with which I had returned.

I'm sure the speaker had good intentions, but he left out an enormous piece. There will be no discipleship fruit when we look at people as an evangelism project. Often our prayer/evangelism list is more about improving our quality of life. We decide these are the people who need to shape up. We make them our personal evangelism projects and they know it.

Of course we want the person to come to Christ for his or her sake. If we are honest, we all have some people in our lives that we wish would be more like Jesus. But is our motivation self-serving? Wouldn't it be great if they were less irritating, or selfish, or rude and dismissive? Our lists usually include people like our spouse, our neighbor, our boss, or the crazy in-laws. We realize that if the person came to Christ, it would improve our quality of life.

While it is natural to want them to change, if the Holy Spirit is not moving them, you can become a negative influence in their lives if you try to do the Spirit's work. If the Spirit is not stirring them, your role is to pray that He will move them. We want ourselves and those we love to avoid pain and difficulty but those are often the circumstances the Spirit uses to move people to seek Him. We must work with the Spirit of God, not work against Him. This approach is very different from "doing evangelism." People get frustrated "doing evangelism" because it seldom works. In this new/old approach we partner with the Spirit of God to do what He wants to accomplish in us.

We become impatient and want to make something happen – or nothing will. Jesus reminds us, in Luke 17:21, that 'The Kingdom of God is in your midst."

God is at work all around us, including in the person you wish would "get it." The critical missing piece is not God's active work, but the person's ability to see God "in their midst." The people you care about will be more inclined to "get it" spiritually when they see how you are being dramatically changed by the transformative work of the Spirit of God.

ITS TIME FOR A NEW APPROACH

First, make a list of people you perceive as being moved by the Holy Spirit. These are the people you need to get to know. Pray about how to build a discipleship relationship with them.

This approach takes all the pressure off us. We don't have to force resistant people to do anything. We don't have to force awkward conversations or pressure anyone. We only have to recognize the people in whom the Spirit is working. It may take a series of spiritual conversations to discover who these people are. In John 3, Jesus said the Spirit is at work all around us. God has put discipleable people in our lives, but we may not be able to recognize them yet. This is a skill to be developed

MAKE A NON-EVANGELISM LIST

Take a moment to write the names in the circles below of those you think are becoming open to the leading of the Holy Spirit.

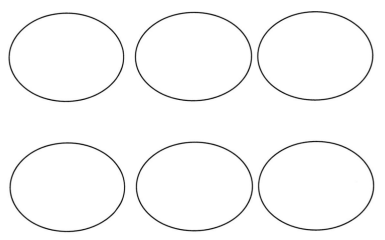

This exercise helps keep us from turning our attentions inward. When we are not intentionally building relationships with discipleable people, it is normal to surround ourselves with safe people. Dealing with people outside of our *oikos* can be messy. When you find discipleable people in a new *oikos*, you will begin to see your world through new eyes. Unfortunately, the longer you've been a Christian, the fewer non-believing friends you have.

Think about the six people you listed in the circles above. How much do you know about their *oikos*? Give the *oikos* a name if you know it and write it above the circle. If they are connected to a soccer club, write "soccer club" above the circle. If they are a hockey mom, write "hockey mom" above the circle.

Identify the *oikos* connection through which you know them, too. Do you know anyone else in their *oikos*? Think about their relationships and *oikos* culture. Take a moment and write to the side if they are a person of peace for their *oikos* group. Write any other helpful information about each person and their *oikos* group.

The Power of Oikos

When we started our churches in southern California, we discovered some *oikos* communities that extended dark tentacles into the lives of people we were reaching. A woman (Sandy) in our new church met another young woman Audrie, (not her real name) and they became good friends. However, Audrie was involved in practices of the occult.

It happened so innocently at first. Audrie had questions about the group but she was on a search for God, hungry to learn and experience. The group also wanted to discuss spiritual things, which fed Audrie's hunger for the supernatural. She soon discovered she had been meeting with a coven of witches.

The group met at a local coffee house near the beach. Members hung out, drank coffee, socialized and kept a low profile. They invited people to discuss spiritual matters. They also regularly met at a theater that had a small bar attached. Everyone showed up at the bar on weekends wearing gothic makeup and dramatic clothing. They had fun going to the theater and watching the midnight showing of cult classics like *The Rocky Horror Picture Show*.

They were fun to be with because they knew all the lines of the movie. When the characters raised a glass and said, "A toast," the group would hurl pieces of toast at the screen. After everyone had a few drinks and hung out for the evening, the group invited Audrie and others to join them for a few drinks.

Audrie knew some of the people had gone a little farther than she was comfortable, but she convinced herself it was innocent fun, even if a little weird. One young woman filed her teeth down to look like vampire fangs. Nonetheless, Audrie liked most of them, and they accepted her.

She eventually discovered this *oikos* had a dark side. Its true nature emerged and she found this was an underground club of vampires, witches and satanists. These people were Audrie's social *oikos*.

At the same time, Audrie was building a relationship with Sandy from our church. Audrie was torn between two very different groups. Sandy got Audrie involved in her discipleship group. Audrie responded to the love and joy she found in the discipleship *oikos.* The more she hung out with them, the more she realized it was God she had been searching for, not the occult practices of those who had embraced her down at the coffee house by the beach. She had been lured in by the power of their dark and twisted *oikos.* The more she got together with Christ followers, the more the Holy Spirit drew her to the things of God.

As Audrie shared her story with our team she said she'd stumbled into the coven of vampires and witches and didn't know how to get out. She didn't realize how much she had allowed them to control her life and thoughts.

Her ability to recognize her spiritual struggle showed signs of progress. She was becoming a follower of Jesus. Before long she repented and opened her life to Christ and the leading of the Holy Spirit. The problem was she was still connected to the coven and wanted to free herself from its grip.

 Nearly everything the coven did was illegal. The more she shared, the more obvious it was how much the satanic rituals and abusive practices had a grip on her soul. We encouraged her simply to leave the coven. She kept saying she wanted to, but she continued to meet with both groups. It was amazing how strong the enemy's grip was on this young woman, using fear and intimidation to keep her in bondage.

The couple discipling Audrie didn't know whether to go to the police and expose the coven, or to prayerfully develop a plan to confront the coven and extract her from its grip. They chose to go more covert.

They prayed and felt they had a plan from the Holy Spirit. They shared the plan with Audrie and she agreed to confront the coven with the help of her new friends. We prayed over the couple and Audrie before they went to face the coven and extract Audrie from its grip.

The power of the God guided the three of them through what could have been a highly tense and confrontational event. They stood toe to toe in the presence of personified evil. The Holy Spirit made a path for Audrie to become a free woman that night.

Audrie's is a story of how a Spirit-directed *oikos* can have a huge impact. God used a discipleship group to provide spiritual freedom for Audrie. God drew her to a group who showed her love and acceptance. They helped her step from bondage into freedom. They helped her learn how to have effective spiritual conversations and to make an impact. She began to share her story of how God gave her freedom and a new life.

The discipleship *oikos* surrounded her and helped her rebuild her life. Audrie learned how to build healthy relationships. She reoriented her relational patterns with men. It wasn't long before she met a young man who also was growing as a transformed Christ follower. They have been married for several years now.

Audrie experienced the powerful bond that happens when an *oikos* comes together. She saw how an *oikos* can be used for evil or for God. When an *oikos* group fights together through a formative experience it can develop a powerful bond. This group's relationships were forged in a trial that tested their faith, and strengthened their conviction in the process.

Audrie grew rapidly once she broke free from the coven. Before long she began to sound like the leaders who were discipling her. She prayed like they did. She began to make disciples like they did. It was completely "caught not taught."

We call this season of rapid spiritual growth a season of spiritual imprinting.

Spiritual Imprinting

I witnessed imprinting growing up on the farm. When a duckling hatched, it naturally imprinted with the first animal larger than itself that it saw. According to enthusiasts at www.thegooses-mother.com no one understands exactly what happens inside a bird's brain when imprinting occurs, but a duckling knows it is the same species as whatever living creature larger than itself it sees upon hatching or shortly thereafter.

"It doesn't *think* it is, it doesn't use the creature for a replacement until it finds its own species, it doesn't pretend to be that species; it *is* that species in its mind," said the author.

We imprint early, too. It's how our life gets oriented. The duckling learns to reproduce the behaviors it sees. Those actions provide the reference point for what it means to be a duck. I have seen a duckling imprint with a little girl. The duckling followed the girl, desperately gathering information for how to grow to the next stage. God made us to imprint both physically and spiritually.

At age one, our granddaughter began to repeat a phrase we had never heard. It sounded like French, but none of us spoke French. My wife noticed that the language cue on the video she played while our granddaughter slept had been moved mistakenly from English to French. All night long while she slept she was learning French. It made perfect sense that she found a way to include the phrase into her vocabulary in perfect context because French had been imprinted into her world.

This happens every time a person comes to Christ, especially if they were not exposed previously to cultural Christianity. The new follower will reproduce whatever is presented to them, either to Jesus or the Church. "Cultural Christians" result when new followers imprint to an institution instead of to the person of Jesus.

The common practice is to expose new followers to church culture as soon as possible, with the objective to turn them into faithful church persons. We want them to "get involved," to serve, give and attend services. Soon they are listening to Christian radio and going only to Christian events. They think, talk and walk like a church person.

Before long their friends ask what happened to them. If they have become a "church disciple" they've likely been prepared to answer that question with a rehearsed speech they're told is "witnessing." The goal is to lead the questioner to repeat a "sinner's prayer," and imprint them to the local church.

Shortly, the new follower has jettisoned his or her previous relationships, and the church imprinting is fully successful. This is the first step of deflating a potentially vibrant and viral disciple maker into a sterile churchgoer who will probably never naturally engage in a starfish movement. This person's only hope for vitality is to detox from the church imprinting process.

In my early pastoral experience I followed that pattern, I'm afraid. I am an evangelist by nature; I have led many people to faith in Christ. For years, after I led someone to Christ I assigned the new believer to someone else to disciple. The new convert often became unmotivated and discouraged.

I grew frustrated because I'd spent a great deal of time building a system that trained disciples to do the follow up with new believers. They were trained to fit into the system I built. But this system never did work very well.

What happened? The new convert had spiritually imprinted to me. This is the problem with "doing evangelism." Mass evangelism is the least effective method of producing disciples. The convert identifies with the evangelist.

But often there is no one with whom to imprint. Odds are they will view their "sinner's prayer" experience as a one-time event and remain in spiritual confusion for a season. Some will take the initiative to join a church. When this happens the church imprints on them and soon they see working in the local church as the highest expression of their spiritual life.

Imprinting is something inherent, placed in a new believer by the Spirit of God. Imprinting provides the relational motivation to care for a new disciple. The bond between a new convert and the person who invested in them to bring them to faith is powerful. I encourage imprinting to occur with the person who will carry out the discipleship process. Paid staff members can't do all the discipleship at any church.

Pulled in Two Directions

I am surprised when church people tell me they really don't know very many non-Christians. It seems to me you would have to go to great lengths to live in a bubble big enough to shut out non-Christians. When church people say they don't know non-Christians they are saying they live in a Christian bubble.

Yet, they live, work and play around non-Christians. Have they found a way to avoid all the irritating pagans in their lives? How did they isolate their church world and their non-Christian worlds from each other ? It takes work to keep those worlds from intersecting.

The cultural Christian church is rapidly dropping from our cultural conscious. The occult, witchcraft and gangs are on the rise because they offer an experience and an embracing *oikos*. People want to experience something meaningful, not just hear about it. The younger generation is not interested in sitting in a sterile building and hearing a seemingly mythical message from long ago. Neil Cole says:

> "The pattern of the modern church used to be: believe, behave, and belong. Today we must see a new pattern where people first belong, then behave, and finally believe. Intellectual assent to a set of propositions is no longer what people want or expect from the collective. They want to associate, belong, and experience the church before any set of propositions is agreed on."[19]

Imbedded in past Christian cultures is a mostly rational belief system where emotions and experience are not to be trusted. The exception is the Pentecostal segment, which is a response to the emotionless "Spock-like" nature of many evangelical Christians. Our culture is on a search for experience. We want to participate and to feel alive.

Modern evangelical Christians are like a person standing with one foot on a dock and the other in a boat that is slowly moving away. Before long you must decide where to stand.

The ideal of *oikos* demands that we break the Christian isolation bubble and re-emerge into the culture. As the two cultures drift farther apart, the temptation increases for Christ followers to isolate and withdraw. In the original starfish movement Christ followers charged head on into the jaws of the enemy.

---

[19]Cole, Neil, Church 3.0, Jossey-Bass Leadership Network Series p. 33-34

They remembered Jesus said: "The gates of hell shall not prevail against it." These uneducated peasants were fearless. They did not retreat when everything in them said to play it safe. They unnerved the Roman elite with their boldness.

They trusted that the Spirit of God would lead them. They knew He would demonstrate His power and life. Jesus didn't leave heaven to start "members only" cliques that would isolate themselves from the world so they could discuss Christian philosophy in cloistered huddles one day a week. He came to start a starfish movement that would break through the "gates of hell."

INSTITUTIONAL SMALL GROUPS WILL BE STERILE

Most of us have been part of a small group in a local church. These groups are formed typically using a programmatic approach that builds groups by putting people together based on certain demographic categories. For example, you usually find groups of singles, young married couples, and couples with preschoolers. These groups are not formed out of natural *oikos*-based relationships.

Jesus trained His followers to think in ways that resulted in reproduction. Leaders in Jesus' time thought in programmatic/institutional ways, too. The problem with institutionally driven small groups is that they almost always are sterile. By sterile, I mean they don't reproduce themselves.

Most small groups have to be maintained and led from an institutional programming level. It requires a staff member to recruit for the small group, to manage the small group, and to provide curriculum for the group to study. They have little energy to think about reproduction.

The anthill leadership church produces sterile non-reproducing small groups. They tend to create groups that focus on serving, and they exist to connect people who have connected to the anthill. The anthill needs a small-group program because there is a felt need for intimacy and community.

The anthill small-group system is the most inefficient small-group model. These groups must be established, maintained and propped up with the institutional muscle of the anthill leader. The leader must champion the small-group ministry. He must staff it, preach about it, and lead it.

The reason these churches struggle to have effective small groups is because the anthill church focus is on the larger group that meets on weekends. The directional leader is the common element among the people in all groups. Most chose the church because they like the leader and the church's direction. These churches often use sermon-based small group discussion to help integrate the small-group experience with the Sunday morning experience.

Their common bond is that everyone attends the anthill on the weekends. The small groups only have a few external things in common, so it tales lots of effort to maintain them so there is little energy for or focus on discipleship reproduction. They use all of their relational energy just getting to know each other.

Small groups have value in our local churches, but we are fooling ourselves if we say they make reproducing disciples. Small groups are excellent at creating community and warm and caring environments. Most small groups are not built to offer the tension necessary for discipleship to occur. At best, small-group leaders facilitate discussion and conversation, not multiplication.

Often people who are new, or who aren't yet Christ followers, can find a small group in which they feel safe and comfortable. It is also an environment that helps to build casual friendships. On some rare occasions, members of such a group can become a close-knit, naturally forming *oikos*. However, most people who join a group don't agree to enter into the kind of discipleship tension that Jesus applied to His disciples, or that is necessary for disciples to be made.

CHAPTER 10

BUILD A NEW
WORLD VIEW

PRINCIPLE FOUR

Every week pastors around the country produce some great sermons with creative elements to hold attention and to demonstrate their points. Even while we've made great strides in communication style from the pulpit, we've seen biblical literacy among the people plummet.

Just 15 years ago you could assume that people in church knew scripture basics. Today we must assume our audience knows very little about the Bible. One researcher has determined that US church attenders are significantly more biblically illiterate now than they were just 25 years ago.[20]

We won't solve this problem by increasing the Bible content in our sermons, or by launching a read-through-the-Bible plan this year. While those are good things to do, the problem is motivation, not information. Attenders have not developed a hunger for scriptural truth because we can't train people to be hungry and "training programs" are the only way we seem to know to address a problem. "You can lead a horse to water, but you can't make him drink," says the old adage.

The only way to change this trend is to create a discipleship environment that produces the kind of tension Jesus created in His disciples' lives. Jesus didn't bemoan the scriptural illiteracy of His day. He created life tension that helped His disciples build a Kingdom of God worldview by motivating them to find answers.

Think back to when you were in school. If you are like me, your motivation to study came from the pressure of pending tests and assignments. I don't remember studying for the sake of learning. Through assignments, the teacher created life tension to motivate us to perform.

I am not recommending that we create homework for those we lead. I am suggesting we do what Jesus did—expose young followers to an introductory level of discipleship tension. Jesus introduced tension when He invited them to follow Him.

---

[20] Biblical Illiteracy in the US at Crisis Point. www.christianpost.com. 2013

"Whoever wants to be my disciple must deny themselves and take up their cross daily and follow me" (Luke 9:23).

He made it clear there would be tension involved in following Him. Later in the same passage, He tells some new disciples:

> "Foxes have dens and birds have nests, but the Son of Man has no place to lay his head..." Still another said, "I will follow you, Lord." Jesus replied, "No one who puts a hand to the plow and looks back is fit for service in the kingdom of God" (Luke 9:58–62).

Jesus introduced tension and challenge, and then progressively increased it. He mixed the challenge with a high dose of love and concern. He also gave them a place to belong.

Then He turned up the tension level by engaging in mild conflict encounters with the Pharisees and Sadducees. This progressed until about the midpoint of His public ministry when He sent His eager followers out in groups of two on a mission to find the "person of peace." He wanted them to understand what was involved in following the leadership of the Spirit.

Being assigned to go into a region with no resources challenged the disciples to apply what they had learned during their brief time with Jesus. I would love to have been a fly on the wall when the disciples returned from their second two-by-two mission. They built skills being away and their numbers had multiplied as well. I'm sure their stories were amazing. It motivated Jesus to declare that this would dethrone Satan from his death grip on humanity.

I also would have loved to hear the questions they had for Jesus. I'm sure the disciples couldn't imagine what came next. In just two years, they would find themselves in the middle of the greatest movement in history. They would witness an unbelievable spiritual outbreak.

For a short season, Jesus absorbed most of the tension and conflict for them. No one can live constantly in the hot seat without a break, so Jesus gave them a brief time to refocus and renew. The disciples had more lessons to learn so they would be prepared for what lay ahead. The next season of instruction probably lasted another year, a year in a protected learning environment before He was crucified, resurrected and ascended to Heaven.

After this, there wouldn't be another chance for one-on-one learning. They would have the Holy Spirit, each other and the *ecclesia* culture He was establishing. Soon they would be the ones who were in the eye of the storm.

Tension Creates Attention

Author Douglas Hyde was influenced in Eastern Europe by the rise of communism, a party that he joined as a young man. His first assignment was to stand on a street corner and hand out communist propaganda. As he distributed his leaflets he encountered people with questions and opposition. He became increasingly anxious because he didn't have a good response to many of the questions. When his two-hour assignment was complete, he hurried to his mentor with lots of questions of his own.

Many years later, Hyde decided to follow Jesus as a disciple. When he came into the church he assumed he would be trained to learn how to make disciples like Jesus did. He had one central question: "Why do the communists make disciples like Jesus, but the church doesn't?"[21]

This is a great question. It reveals how far we have drifted from the commission of Jesus to "Go make disciples." We have drifted because most of us have not been discipled to make disciples.

Douglas Hyde's experience illustrates why discipleship does not happen in most of our churches – there is little discipleship tension. Disciples are never created accidentally. Discipleship is an intentional pursuit.

Jesus' response to some people who volunteered to follow Him confused me for years. It seemed He would turn down potential followers. In Luke 9:57 a man came wanting to follow Jesus as a disciple, but Jesus did not offer him a next step.

As I mentioned before, only motivated disciples could follow Him. A few verses later, Jesus confronted another candidate on his financial plan to receive a double inheritance. He counseled the man not to trust in the extra income he could gain by staying on the family farm and being executor of his dad's inheritance.

---

[21] Doulas Hyde, *Red Star Versus the Cross: The Pattern of Persecution*, Paternoster Publications, London, 1954. p.89

Jesus challenged him not to miss out on the discipleship adventure that awaited him.

"Let the dead bury their own dead," Jesus said, meaning that He was sure the man had a brother who would be glad to earn the executor fee to administrate the estate. He told the man to follow Him and trust the Heavenly Father to provide. It was an invitation to trust Jesus for the things we typically worry and fret about. He explained this journey is not for the faint of heart.

If your image of discipleship is attending classes at church, it's no wonder Christians don't understand why Jesus made such a big deal about the cost of discipleship.

The best way to introduce discipleship tension is to do what Jesus did. Jesus didn't try to start anything on a national scale. He started the process the way you build a campfire.

If you have ever started a campfire in the woods, you know the drill. You start with finding the right environment, a dry area protected from the wind. Next, you gather kindling and a few small, dry twigs, and place all of the starter elements close by. Light the match and carefully feed the small, fragile flame dry kindling. Little by little you introduce a few dry leaves, then some twigs, then some small branches. Before long your little match has become a roaring campfire.

Jesus chose to work among fishermen. Even though the temple was only 100 miles south, fishermen were far removed from the Jewish culture in Jerusalem. They probably had seldom, if ever, attended a religious event in Jerusalem. They were not candidates for rabbinic training. They were ritually unclean, according to Jewish law. But Jesus identified them as candidates who would "catch fire" quickly. He had all the elements needed to launch a roaring campfire of a movement.

First, He selected the right location; second, He moved to Capernaum on the northern shore of the Sea of Galilee. He launched His first group with the handful of followers who were discipleable. Then He began to cultivate the new culture. It started as a spark, and grew.

If we want to experience what the disciples experienced, we must do what Jesus did. Our efforts must start small. Most church planters start by organizing a worship gathering. Instead, start with a small *oikos*-based group of discipleable people. If these people come from a church background, they will probably need some help moving from the toxic Christian culture to a starfish-multiplication culture. I recommend launching an Xcellerate gathering.

If you are interested in launching this process, I recommend you begin by enrolling in the Generate intensive-training process where you will learn how to launch an Xcellerate gathering out of your local church setting. These gatherings will create a multiplication culture that will birth a series of groups designed to rapidly multiply disciples. We call these X-groups.

X-groups are same-sex groups of three to six people who meet regularly to reproduce disciples. Participants are identified by leaders looking for discipleable people willing to build a biblical worldview. They begin each meeting discussing their spiritual conversations from the prior week.

Spiritual conversations produce the tension that motivates them to explore the Scriptures. Group members will discuss what they have uncovered while wrestling with the tensions of the past week. A high degree of accountability is required for how the disciples are walking with Jesus each week. This will include a review of how they are advancing in the area of identifying and cultivating other discipleable people – and a time for honest confession of sin.

When they encounter skeptics who push back, the X-group leader will help the new disciple search the Scriptures for answers, and find adequate response to the tension. They will discuss the tension that naturally emerges between the secular world and a biblical perspective. These groups encourage and challenge each other as they probe the Scriptures to construct new reference points for living. They learn a better understanding of how to have an authentic spiritual life in this new Kingdom culture.

Tension is Necessary for Us to Learn

So, while churches say, "We do discipleship in our small groups," the fact is most small groups are missing the key ingredient of discipleship tension required to launch a discipleship culture.

Small groups have value. People can find relationships and build friendships there, but biblical discipleship doesn't happen particularly well. Most small groups resist homework and challenge. The motivation for small-group attendance is socially based—most simply want to get to know some people in the church.

But discipleship tension is necessary for us to develop as healthy disciples. Soon after Columbia University built the Biosphere Center in Oracle, Arizona, the 3.1-acre greenhouse and research laboratory in the desert began to experience some problems. Scientists expected the fruit grown there to set records for growth. They assumed that if you remove all the pests and threats, and give plants and trees all the nourishment that they need, growth records would result.

However, before long, the fruit began falling off the trees before it had fully ripened. After investigating, they discovered a startling fact. Because the perfect, protected environment had shielded the fruit trees from wind, rain and harsh elements of nature their branches didn't strengthen enough to hold the fruit until it reached full maturity.[22]

When we experience tension in our lives, God will use it to grow and strengthen us as His disciples. Personal tension creates the ability for us to listen to the Holy Spirit.

People seem to grow best when they are in tension. Likewise, when the church is in tension, it stays focused on what matters

---

[22] Robert D. Dale. Cultivating Perennial Churches: TCP Kindle Location684-688.

most. When Rick Warren gathered his church planters, he told us, "Remember to stay focused on your mission. Keep them focused on the mission, because the mission matters. Nobody complains on the front lines of war. They are focused on the enemy. It's when you get off of the front lines that everyone starts to complain. When churches lose their focus, they create personal conflict." Keep your culture focused on the mission and aware of the enemy, and you will not have unnecessary conflict in your church.

Have you noticed that movements seem to occur more easily in places and times of severe persecution? Neil Cole suggests that when the church is persecuted, it seems to thrive. "Perhaps it's because the church is not able to do the things that hinder a movement such as hiring professionals, buying and maintaining facilities, creating programs, and offering religious services. Without these distractions, rapid and spontaneous movements can emerge."[23]

When a persecuted church is stripped of the resources needed to fund and staff these distractions or peripheral acts of devotion and faith, Christ becomes more real. In these situations they embrace their relationship with Jesus and often a movement results. When movement impediments are removed the Spirit of God is free to move unchecked and with great power.

Perhaps you are asking, "Can we see this happen in our setting?" We are seeing opposition toward Christ followers increase even

[23]Neil Cole, Church 3.0 Jossey Bass, San Francisco, CA P 68

here in the U.S. Resistance has been rising internationally for some time. If resistance to Christ continues to rise, God will use this discipleship tension to help us make disciples. God will use this tension to build His church.

Starfish

CHAPTER 11

Reproduce the Culture

PRINCIPLE FIVE

When I was ten years old, a friend gave me two rabbits for Easter. I brought them home and announced I was going into the rabbit raising business. These two rabbits were going to seed the start of a rabbit empire that would rule the world.

Well, they didn't end up ruling the world, but they did their best to populate it. I realized why my friend was so willing to give away rabbits.

I had to mow yards to buy rabbit food. My rabbit business was all overhead and no profit. Nobody was interested in buying my product. I guess rabbit meat was not in high demand. When I tried to give them away, everybody just laughed. By mid summer I already had built three pens and this thing was out of control. A rabbit's gestation period is just 28 days. This means a rabbit can have baby rabbits 12 times a year. A female can get pregnant when it's six months old and it can live up to nine years.

You get the picture. They are reproduction machines. A rabbit can reproduce because it is a simple creature with a simple skeletal system built to reproduce. Rabbits are simple in every way.

If you took a male and a female rabbit and a male and a female elephant and placed both pairs in their natural environment with all the food and water they need, in 36 months there would be three elephants and literally millions of rabbits.[24]

Elephants are very different from rabbits. They are complex creatures with a gestation period of nearly two years. Their skeletons take months to form. The more complex anything is – from an animal to a scientific formula – the harder it is to reproduce. That same principle is true when it comes to our church culture.

Jesus established a simple movement designed to reproduce rapidly. He reduced complexity because the more complex things are the slower they reproduce.

---

[24] George Bara, Audrie & Felicity Dale, Tyndale, Brentwood, TN p.12

Is your church simple or complex? That is an important question. Most American churches are complex operations, making them less flexible and adaptable. Our U.S. church discipleship model looks more like that of the Pharisees and Sadducees than that of Jesus. They created a system that was top down, like a government bureaucracy. Complex organizations protect themselves and consolidate their power.

Jesus established a starfish movement that would have no head but Him, and they were not to have power struggles. In Mark 10:42, He said, "You know that those who are regarded as rulers of the Gentiles lord it over them, and their high officials exercise authority over them. Not so with you."

Jesus' system was so simple a person could catch the culture quickly and immediately begin to reproduce the culture. Have you built an anthill culture that requires constant work to maintain? Do you have to hire people to manage it because it's simply too much for volunteers? That is a major departure from the starfish movement.

In the New Testament, individuals who led the churches were only months before far from Christ. Some even had been hostile to the movement. They had little training but quickly discovered when they reproduced disciples they naturally became leaders of those disciples and at the head of a new church movement. It was normal for a Christ follower to grow rapidly and reproduce communities of new Christ followers.

Reproduction should be a natural early step of discipleship. The Holy Spirit specializes in using people who know they don't have the answers and are hungry for His help. The Holy Spirit is a skilled coach, and Jesus called Him the "comforter." The Holy Spirit is a constant presence in every situation.

Jesus had not been gone long before things started to heat up for His followers. Acts 8 says persecution broke out and everyone scattered. The story focuses on Philip, who was in the middle of the country. "The Angel of the Lord said to Philip, go south, go down from Jerusalem to Gaza" (Acts 8:26). Philip simply obeyed. He had a divine appointment.

Then the Spirit said Philip would see a chariot and he was to go to it. Philip ran up to the chariot and started a spiritual conversation with the Ethiopion driver. The conversation progressed so well that we see the driver becoming a disciple. The driver learned all he could in a short time and was on his way. Obviously, he made reproducing disciples because in a short time, the Church emerged in Africa. The Ethiopian went from his encounter with Philip, on to Africa armed only with some Old Testament prophesies about Jesus and a new relationship with the Holy Spirit.

This is a great case study for letting the Spirit lead you to find a "person of peace." The Holy Spirit led Philip to a discipleable person. He quickly cultivated that person and began to disciple him in the short time he had. God obviously had gone before

Philip and prepared the man's heart for discipleship. Philip remembered the process of Jesus' instructions.

Philip started the process with a question, asking the man if he understood what he was reading. There was no mention of a formal commitment, or formulaic prayer being recited. Philip merely prepared him to believe and multiply.

As related in the New Testament, that is one of the more hurried discipleship encounters we will find. Chances are Philip spent the day with him in an intense discipleship encounter, teaching and eventually baptizing him. The Ethiopian was unfamiliar with scripture and had learned no systematic theology or apologetics so he could fight over shades of meaning with other Christ followers. In this story there are none of the elements we use to sterilize new followers.

I don't know why the Spirit took Philip away from his new convert so quickly. But I do know He wants to establish in our lives a dependency on Him that is far more than a dependency on a person, or an institution, or a curriculum. He wants us to know He can use a new convert to reach a continent. I also know the Spirit is leading us to go personally on mission to learn how to better trust His leading in our lives.

Jesus taught us to begin the process of discipling first, before a person is converted, counted and baptized. This approach is not attractive to the institutional church because it's hard to measure or celebrate. We can be overly eager to celebrate decisions for Christ. Often these decisions don't result in much spiritual fruit.

If Christ followers are taught to disciple first and allow the fruit to form, they will discover that discipleship and life transformation will explode in their midst.

THEY NEED TO BE DISCIPLED BUT SAY THEY WANT TO BE FED?

Church leaders get frustrated when people say they need to go to a church that will feed them. That is an odd thing to say. I don't ever remember asking to be fed. The only two groups who need to be fed are infants and the infirm.

U.S. church members have heard it said so often they just repeat the same tired phrase. This idea comes from a misguided understanding that associates information transfer with maturity. Frustrated preachers offer up complex messages to meet this request. They have instituted the finest training classes, special events and seminars, yet people still say they need "to find a place that will feed them." No amount of programming or training will offer the same satisfaction and growth as reproducing a disciple who will multiply other disciples.

If a person never uses what they have learned, spiritual atrophy sets in. Think of the phrase, "Use it or lose it."

My family keeps a sponge on the edge of our sink. One day I grabbed it to wipe up a spill, but it just pushed the spill around. The sponge had been doing its job beautifully, but proper sponge care requires that it be wrung out. When Christ followers soak up information without ever being wrung out, they eventually cease to absorb any more and become useless.

God designed us to make a difference, not just to absorb information. Absorbing massive amounts of information without putting your learning into action is dangerous. It will shift your focus to "doing the right thing" instead of growing as disciple-making followers.

What is missing in the "info soak" school is the contagious nature of replication that Jesus brought. A new convert will naturally repeat the process that drew him or her to Christ with another person who is far from Christ. It's contagious. Remember, simple things reproduce; complex things have to be maintained because they break easily.

I remember seeing the Disney movie *Peter Pan* as a kid. The main character is an impish little boy who can fly and wears green tights. This kid never grows up. He lives with buddies on the small island of Neverland, interacting with Indians, fairies and pirates in a perpetual state of childhood.

This describes the spiritual condition of too many folks in our churches. They have matured into adulthood in every area except in their spiritual lives. They rely on one person to tell them what to think about the Bible. They depend on this person for their motivation.

Their spiritual growth is stunted at the adolescence stage. They never move on to the challenging and exciting stage of reproduction. The longer they remain in spiritual "Neverland," the harder it is for them to break out and live a more productive, fulfilling and satisfying spiritual life. It seldom occurs to them that personal spiritual growth happens when we reproduce.

Think about your own life. When did you grow the most as an adult? It was likely when you took the first step of leaving home, going to college or getting your own place near work. It's scary, isn't it, but so exciting, too. Then graduation approaches and you're forced again to step into "the great unknown." These are growth times you would never experience if you just continued to sit and soak and never wrung yourself out with a new challenge.

CHAPTER 12

Develop a Singular Focus

TO LAUNCH A STARFISH MOVEMENT

Have you seen a lion tamer work?

With no more than a stool and a whip they control a ferocious 400-pound, muscular beast with sharp claws and teeth. This king of the jungle is the apex predator. Of all the defensive mechanisms at hand, I've always wondered why lion tamers choose a stool and a whip. It seems like a gun and a Kevlar suit might be safer choices. As it turns out the two traditional tools are all the lion tamer needs.

Lions become distracted and passive when presented with multiple objects on which to focus, like the stool's three legs and the whip's crack. If the trainer in the cage was the only thing on which the lion had to focus, it would be much more aggressive. This is an important principle for us to learn.

By design, churches have created an environment that prompts attendees to become passive. New believers are focused on one thing: the Jesus who changed their lives. When they connect with a church, the distractions of "doing church" naturally makes them passive.

After a month on his journey, one young Christ follower said, "These people want me to be a Republican who works at a church service three times a week. They expect me to give a chunk of my money away, and require me to change how I talk and dress." That's a lot to process.

He said, "I just wanted to follow Jesus. I had no idea all of this was ahead when I made that decision."

Most churches have become so complex that the leaders and staff struggle to articulate mission in the local church.

Churches create passive attendees oriented away from real action when they create environments with too many distractions. I recently attended a worship service in which four different challenges were presented. During the week, attendees were to attend a small group that studied a completely different topic. They then had a mid-week worship event that presented three more ideas. So this church presented eight different things for its attendees to consider that week. And that church considers itself a simple church!

Just a few short years ago, typical churches had a Sunday School hour on Sunday morning before the worship service. They then had another training hour before Sunday evening services, a Wednesday evening service, a host of committee meetings, and other events for each member of the family. It was ridiculous.

A person could be presented with as many as 30 different challenges in a single week. These kinds of busy churches distracted their attendees from the mission of Jesus. People already are overwhelmed with a flood of information to process every day. Our daily information input is greater than the total amount of information a person received in a lifetime just 120 years ago.[25]

Jesus challenged His followers to embrace one primary challenge. Embrace the Kingdom of God, and make disciples who will live under Kingdom authority.

Our over-programming in the midst of an information explosion has resulted in a passive Christian culture – like the over stimulated lion. Christian pastors/teachers tend to make the simple complex. Perhaps they do it to create job security?

[25]Avery T Willis Jr, and Mark Snowden, *Truth that Sticks,* (Nav Press, Colorado Springs Colorado , 2010),

How many times have you heard that someone "is deep?" Should that be a compliment? Maybe it's just that the speaker makes everything sound complicated, not easily understood, and therefore "deep." When we keep it simple, ordinary people will be encouraged to attempt it. This is the only way to release the power of the starfish movement.

What would happen if every Christ follower embraced the starfish principle? What if each began to realize they could make disciples, care for them and baptize them? What if they took on the role of primary caregiver for the disciples they were developing? The focus would shift from the professional, paid Christian and empower the starfish disciple maker.

THERE IS A PLACE FOR EVERYONE

A key step is to develop a singular focus in your spiritual life. The Holy Spirit will use every personality and gift to launch a starfish culture. It doesn't matter what kind of leader you are, there is a place for you.

In the book of Acts, Paul and his team identified discipleable people and helped them reach their *oikos*. They then left the area and churches bloomed behind them. In every case, it wasn't the apostles who made things happen. The movement continued because of the local non-apostolic/directional leaders. Ephesians 4 tells us that God has established five primary kinds of leaders for His *ecclesia*/church.

The first is the apostle. The other four are the ones who continue the starfish movement after the apostle has moved on. They are described as prophets, evangelists, shepherds and teachers. It appears to me that the groups who do the best job of developing a reproduction movement are the shepherds and teachers.

Shepherds tend to stabilize and care for the movement. These leaders transform what would have been a one-and-done event into an ongoing, fruitful ministry because they support and care for the people.

A starfish movement needs all five leadership styles. Consider both Paul and Timothy. The Apostle Paul was essential for the movement to multiply to the "ends of the earth." But early on, Paul knew he needed to transfer leadership to the next generation as soon as he could.

In the New Testament epistles, we see the names of many leaders who followed Paul. Most did not have the gifting of an apostlic/directional leader. There were a few exceptions like Titus. Most of Paul's traveling companions tended to be more in the vein of evangelist, shepherd or teacher. There were 19 total disciples who traveled with Paul at one time or another to plant churches. Among those who had shepherding qualities were Barnabas, Silas, Timothy and Epaphras, to name a few. Paul would leave some of these men behind to establish the church, and he would continue on as an apostolic/directional leader.

It's an essential part of leadership development to give away your job. If not, things stagnate Every disciple must find someone who can carry on the movement. This process creates leadership growth for both the disciple and the apostolic/directional leader. We commonly pass on the torch only when we are unable to carry it any longer. Instead, we need to do it as a part of our leadership development strategy.

Paul knew Timothy's character and saw that he had a strong capacity to lead. Even though Timothy was young, he carried a great spiritual load. Paul said in his second letter to Timothy, chapter one, verse seven: "For God did not give us a spirit of timidity, but a spirit of power, of love and self-discipline."

Paul encouraged Timothy to follow up on discipleship. In 2 Timothy 1:5–6 Paul wrote, "Fan into flame the gift of God, which is in you."

Paul like Jesus, invested in leaders who were disciple-able. Timothy was open, coachable, and ready to follow Jesus.

Paul challenged Timothy to ignite into the kind of leader he knew Timothy could be. Paul's goal was for Timothy to take action and create a culture of discipleship in the city of Ephesus, and the surrounding region.

Paul gave us a glimpse into how he coached Timothy with these words of encouragement in 2 Timothy 2:2:

"And the things you have heard me say in the presence of many witnesses entrust to reliable people who will also be qualified to teach others."

Paul helped Timothy see what a multiplying culture would look like with the power to ripple into four generations of leaders. He coached Timothy to invest in "reliable people." A strong leader will attract other leaders who will attract followers.

You can have two "generations" of influence without ever multiplying. To get to the fourth generation of disciples, leaders must empower the next generation. This is the only way we will ever multiply and inaugurate a starfish culture.

> *Timothy quickly embraced the culture of multiplication, because it had become the new normal for him. We will experience the multiplication of disciples when the starfish culture becomes the new normal for those we are discipling.*

Paul knew how easy it is to get distracted and lose focus. He challenged Timothy to reproduce himself because making new disciples would provide the stimulation Timothy needed to continue multiplying. Paul knew getting Timothy to be a multiplying disciple was going to take some coaching, because we tend to settle for growth by addition. Whether or not the way of Jesus would become a movement was in Timothy's hands. Paul knew it wouldn't happen if Timothy held onto the leadership reins and didn't empower the next generation of leaders.

CHAPTER 13

LEARN TO QUIT WELL

LAUNCHING A STARFISH MOVEMENT

One brisk October afternoon, when I was in third grade, I came home from piano lessons and announced I was quitting. Mom tried to dissuade me by telling me Aesop's fable about the race between the tortoise and the hare. She even acted it out for me.

After sprinting out to a big lead, the hare was so confident of winning he took a nap midway through the race. But when the hare awoke the steady, the determined tortoise already had crawled across the finish line.

Mom combined this story with some Vince Lombardi wisdom to drive home the point that "winners never quit, and quitters never win." Despite her best theatrical effort, I still quit piano lessons so I could play basketball.

Don't let my decision reflect poorly on my mom's ability to tell a good story! I just decided to quit. I never did learn to play the piano. Nevertheless, I did learn the value of quitting something that isn't working.

Mom was wrong; winners actually quit all the time. They simply learn to quit the right things at the right times. Most people quit something, but few know how to quit successfully. Quitting one thing is the only way to create new capacity to do another thing that is more important to you.

The lesson never to give up is important, once you have locked in on your sole focus, but we get in trouble when we apply this principle too generally. Jesus quit almost everything the Jewish religious culture deemed valuable so he could create the bandwidth to start a discipleship movement.

With Jesus as our example, we see that learning to quit well is a valuable skill to possess. Most of us who engage in disciple-making have not quit enough other peripheral activities to focus on making disciples. Too many programs and events compete for our attention. If we are over committed we will never get enough traction to launch a starfish movement.

RESPOND TO FATIGUE
BY LEARNING TO QUIT

Being heavily committed to extraneous causes, programs and events will leave you exhausted. In that case, you don't need a tortoise and hare pep talk. You don't need someone to tell you to buckle down and run faster. You're fatigued because you haven't learned to quit well. What is competing with your primary purpose of reproducing disciples?

There are two types of quitting: reactive and strategic. Reactive quitting is the trademark of those who jump on the latest trend or hot new program. Their pattern is to start new projects easily but only half finish them. This is a common pattern of a leader who is tired, fatigued or discouraged.

I learned the lesson of strategic quitting around year eight of the church plant in Southern California. I realized we were in trouble when our discipleship leaders became distracted and unmotivated. They showed signs of ministry exhaustion that I attribute to a lack of singular focus. They were overwhelmed and were neglecting their disciples.

Morale dropped. The leaders made excuses for not following up on their discipling relationships. The discipleship culture suddenly became unstable.

I thought we had simplified as much as we could. After all, we were one of the churches Tom Rainer had researched for his book *Simple Church*. Our leaders didn't want us to cut anything we were doing. On the outside, things were humming and I told myself we would get through this. But the leaders were showing signs of serious stress fractures.

I began to pray about what to do. The Holy Spirit, along with my wife (I get those two confused sometimes), prompted me to be ruthless in cutting back on many activities. We needed to stop doing so many things as a church. Some leaders were already self-selecting out. When the culture is over stimulated, leaders will adopt a self-preservation mode to protect themselves.

This is a sign they are not being led well. Your leaders will tell you how much they can handle, not through what they say, but by how they behave.

No one had the courage to say we needed to cut the biggest thing we do all spring. Our Easter event was the single most effective thing we did to raise our profile in the community. We pulled out all the stops. We combined our services and held a large outdoor event that drew more than 4,000 people.

For nearly a decade, our outdoor Easter service held in a flower field on a hillside overlooking the Pacific Ocean had been the single most defining event we did as a church. We were known as the church that did Easter in the flower fields. We were featured on news stations in San Diego and Los Angeles; and in articles in the *LA Times,* the *Union Tribune,* and the *Wall Street Journal.* This event was amazingly successful.

But, as great as things had been, we were at a crisis point. Clearly, if we didn't simplify we could lose much of our discipleship culture. Would I depend on what had worked in the past? How would we define ourselves if we dropped the special Easter service? This potential change could alter our identity as a church, and my identity as pastor of the church that did Easter in the flower fields. This was a huge issue for me as a leader.

Looking back on it now, I see how the Holy Spirit was discipling *me.* If I had clung to past experience and sacrificed the discipleship culture, it would have been a tragic mistake. Still, there was no guarantee that God would continue to move in the amazing ways He had been moving if I made a change.

I expected the leaders to be shocked when I asked them to pray about dropping the special Easter service. But it was immediately obvious the event was far more important to me than it was to anyone else. I was at first disturbed about how few people seemed attached to it.

More than that, I was stunned at what happened almost immediately after we decided not to do the production. A cloud of frustration lifted, making room in our culture to do what was most important. It had a huge impact. After all, I had repeatedly taught that Jesus asked us to make disciples. Canceling the event gave us margin in our schedules, and it communicated how serious we were about making disciples.

There is power in quitting well. It was counter-intuitive to back off one of the very things that had resulted in great ministry success but it was obviously what the Spirit of God was leading us to do. In the season that followed we birthed four church plants and saw many more disciples engage in multiplication.

By the way, one of our new church plants began doing Easter in the flower fields. It has produced a great season of ministry for them.

Training to Expand
The Starfish Movement

Our organization's training events are called Generate Intensives (generatedisciples.com). The focus is helping people establish a discipleship culture that generates disciples to the fourth generation. It's probably not legitimate to use the term *starfish movement* until disciples are reproducing to the fourth generation.

After a person has been exposed to the ideas in Generate One, we allow a little time for those ideas to germinate. If leaders decide to take the next step, they can attend Generate Two training. To prepare for this level, a leader must take a small group of his most influential culture-shapers through our online training course and read this book.

During this training leaders learn the principles for launching multiplication cultures in their own communities. We follow up with coaching and monthly online training sessions.

Leaders who implement the principles and launch starfish cultures get invited to our next level – Generate Three – training. This teaches leaders how to expand the movement and to launch a public worship event.

We constantly train new leaders by engaging them in the training process. Everyone learns more by teaching than by being taught. We usually have at least two presenters for each training class.

By getting more leaders involved, we expand our ability to launch more starfish movements. At first the trainers only tell a few stories and answer questions with "color commentary." The next time, they teach a little more and take the lead during certain parts. By the third or fourth time through, the leaders are ready to be presenters with new apprentices. This process allows the culture to expand and multiply.

The Heart of the Movement

Braveheart is an all-time movie favorite for many. One of its main characters, Robert the Bruce, was a fiery Scottish noble who took up the mantle of leadership after William Wallace was executed. In *The Barbarian Way*, Erwin McManus tells this story as a mixture of history and legend.

> "Shortly before his death, Robert the Bruce requested that his heart be removed from his body and taken on a crusade by a worthy knight. One of his closest friends was at his bedside and took on the responsibility. The heart of Robert the Bruce was embalmed and placed in a

small container that Douglas carried around his neck. In every battle that Douglas fought, he literally carried the heart of his king pressed up against his chest.

"In the early spring of 1330, Douglas sailed from Scotland to Granada, Spain, and engaged in a campaign against the Moors. In an ill-fated battle, Douglas found himself surrounded, and in this situation death was both certain and imminent. In that moment, Douglas reached for the heart strapped around his neck, flung the heart into the enemy's midst, and cried out, 'Fight for the heart of your king!'

"One historian quoted Douglas as shouting, 'Forward, brave heart, as ever thou were wont to do, and Douglas will follow his king's heart or die.' To this day, the motto of the Douglas clan, to which the present duke belongs, is simply 'Forward Brave Heart!'"[26]

The strength of the movement is to follow the heart of the one who initiated it. If you know the heart of Jesus, you know it's a call to follow Him. He invites us to leave everything and follow. You will feel His heart beat in your chest and hear His voice within crying out: "Forward Brave Heart. Fight for the heart of your king!" The heart of our King beats in all who have breathed in the Spirit of God.

To embrace the starfish movement is to embrace the heart of Jesus. To be faithful to the commission to which He has called us

---

[26]Erwin McManus, *The Barbarian Way*, 2-4.

requires that we shed distractions and our own ambitions. Jesus gave this enormous mission to ordinary people like us. That's why the starfish movement is within the grasp of anyone who will take up the challenge Jesus laid down 2,000 years ago, to "make disciples" as we go about our lives.

"The idea of this idea that we could launch a movement would be laughable, if not for this final observation. Anyone looking at the 11 disciples and hearing Jesus' commission would have thought this work was dead in the water before it had ever begun. How on earth could an intelligent person such as Jesus think that a motley crew of misfits such as these fishermen and tax collectors could carry out such a huge plan?

"Indeed, the idea would be foolish if not for the opening and closing words of the passage. Jesus begins with the words "All authority has been given to Me in heaven and on earth." It is not "a lot of authority"; it isn't even "most authority"; it is "all authority."[27]

We *will* be able to lead the movement God has placed in our hearts. Why? Because He has given us all the power we need to accomplish the task. Remember, the One who commissioned you is the One who has been given all authority on earth and in heaven. Therefore, go!

---

[27]Neil Cole. "Search & Rescue, Baker Books, Grand Rapids, MI P151."

Crucial Conversations

Is available for **$11 each**
Plus $5 shipping and handling per book

Order at
IgniteDiscipleship.com
or send payment to
Po Box 70632
Knoxville, TN 37938

Differences divide. We get that. If you've ever wondered why it seems a chasm separates you from people you'd like to engage in conversation, you're not alone.

If you're uncomfortable talking about your faith, this book gives you tools to bridge the awkward chasm and initiate conversations crucial to helping people take an initial faith step.

Learning the practical ideas, examples and icons in these pages will give you confidence to bridge the spiritual gap. Jesus initiated vibrant crucial conversations with a broad range of people who thought differently than He did. We study how He did it to help you engage in honest, open, crucial conversations without awkwardness.

Case price **$9 each** in Cases of 10
Plus $15 Shipping and Handling per case

Is available for **$11 each**
Plus $5 shipping and handling per book

Order at
IgniteDiscipleship.com
or send payment to
Po Box 70632
Knoxville, TN 37938

Case price **$9 each** in Cases of 10
Plus $15 Shipping and Handling per case

UNLEASHING   THE   UNSTOPPABLE